QUICK & EASY MIXOLOGY

GARDEN of GRAPES.

First Edition: 2024

Published by Garden of Grapes.

Printed in USA

Library of Congress Cataloging-in-Publication Data:

First edition.
Includes index.

Manufactured in USA

Introduction

Ladies and gentlemen, wanderers of the spirits and seekers of liquid alchemy, welcome to the hallowed pages of "Quick & Easy Mixology." In these intoxicating realms, where libations become poetry, I extend my hand in camaraderie.

This isn't just a mixology; it's a journey through the art of crafting the perfect cocktail—a symphony of flavors and fables poured into every glass. As we embark on this spirited escapade, envision an intoxicating blend of inspiration and dedication, shaken not stirred.

Why cocktails, you might ask? Well, my friends, the answer is simple: life is too short for mediocre drinks. In the hazy swirl of a well-mixed libation, there's a story—a tale of flavors dancing in harmony, a narrative that unfolds in every sip.

My inspiration for this endeavor? Picture the crowded, dimly lit bars, the clinking of ice against glass, the laughter punctuating the air. It's a celebration of the craft, a homage to the bartenders who transform spirits into liquid poetry. Their passion became my muse, and "Quick & Easy Mixology" is my ode to the cocktail culture that transcends time and trends.

Now, as you thumb through these pages, expect more than just a list of recipes. This is a curated selection of libations, each with its own personality, born from the fusion of spirits, mixers, and a dash of audacity. From classic concoctions that have weathered the ages to contemporary elixirs that push the boundaries, you'll find a repertoire that suits both the novice and the seasoned mixologist.

Whether you're shaking up a storm for a soirée or crafting a quiet nightcap for yourself, this book is your compass in the vast seas of mixology. Each recipe is a portal to a different dimension of taste, a chance to elevate your home bar game with minimal effort and maximum flair.

So, dear readers, brace yourselves for a journey where the shaker is your compass, the glass your canvas, and the spirits your muse. "Quick & Easy Mixology" is more than a guide; it's an invitation to elevate your libation game and embrace the artistry of crafting unforgettable moments, one sip at a time. Cheers to the alchemy of spirits and the tales spun in every well-poured drink.

Mixing Philosophy or Approach

In the realm of spirited concoctions and liquid alchemy lies "Quick & Easy Mixology," a libation compendium curated with a dash of audacity and a measure of irreverence—because, let's face it, cocktails are not just drinks; they're stories in a glass, waiting to be uncorked.

My philosophy? It's simple: Liberation in libation. This is not a book of tedious formulas but a celebration of the liquid arts. No need for a degree in mixology; just a spirit of adventure and the willingness to bend a few rules.

Here, we delve into the uncharted territories of flavor, where classic meets contemporary, and the boundaries of tradition are meant to be blurred. It's about crafting concoctions that tell tales, that make your taste buds dance a jig of delight.

Techniques? Think of it as a cocktail cabaret. We shake, stir, muddle, and swizzle with abandon. From the precise elegance of a stirred martini to the fiery flair of a flamboyant garnish, each technique is a brushstroke on the canvas of liquid imagination.

Ingredients? We're not just talking about spirits and mixers. We're talking about infusions, tinctures, and garnishes that elevate a drink from a mere sip to a symphony. Fresh herbs, exotic fruits, and unexpected spices—these are the secret weapons in our arsenal.

Styles? Oh, we've got them all. Whether you're in the mood for a timeless classic or a contemporary creation that defies conventions, there's a recipe waiting to be poured into your glass. Tiki vibes, prohibition-era elegance, or a modern twist on a familiar favorite—you're the director of your liquid narrative.

In the spirit of fearless approach to cuisine, this book is a call to embrace the unconventional, to break free from the shackles of the ordinary and embark on a liquid odyssey. So, gather your tools, stock your bar, and let's mix up some magic. After all, life's too short for bland drinks and predictable flavors. Cheers to crafting the perfect cocktail, one rebellious pour at a time.

Tips for Successful Mixing

Welcome to the world of 'Quick & Easy Mixology,' where we're not just shaking cocktails; we're stirring up a symphony of flavors that dance on your palate. But before you embark on this liquid adventure, let's talk about the backbone of any good concoction - the art of successful mixology.

Tips for Successful Cocktail Crafting:

1. Quality Over Quantity: Just like in life, it's about quality, not quantity. Invest in premium spirits, fresh fruits, and top-notch mixers. Your taste buds will thank you.

2. Ice, Ice, Baby: Ice isn't just for cooling; it's for dilution and creating the perfect balance. Invest in good ice cubes, or better yet, get creative with ice molds to elevate your drink presentation.

3. Tools of the Trade: A mixologist is only as good as their tools. Invest in a sturdy shaker, a jigger for precise measurements, and a muddler to coax the flavors out of your ingredients.

4. Fresh is Best: Embrace the bounty of nature. Freshly squeezed citrus juices, handpicked herbs - these little touches make all the difference.

5. Balance is Key: A great cocktail is a delicate dance of flavors. Strive for balance between sweetness, acidity, bitterness, and alcohol. It's the sweet spot where magic happens.

6. Garnish with Purpose: Garnishes aren't just for show; they're the finishing touch. Citrus twists, herbs, or even a well-placed edible flower can elevate your cocktail from good to exceptional.

7. Experiment & Improvise: The best mixologists are fearless experimenters. Don't be afraid to tweak recipes, substitute ingredients, or invent your own concoctions. It's your palate - trust it.

Now, armed with these tips, dive into the pages of "Quick & Easy Mixology." Each recipe is a canvas, waiting for your personal touch. Remember, it's not just about making a drink; it's about crafting an experience, one sip at a time.

So, grab your shaker, measure with precision, and let the alchemy of mixology unfold. May your cocktails be as bold as your spirit and as unforgettable as the memories they create. Cheers to the art of crafting the perfect cocktail!

Bar Essentials

In the alchemical realm of "Quick & Easy Mixology," where spirits dance and glasses clink, we find ourselves standing at the Bar's threshold. Before we dive into the symphony of cocktails, lets talk about the unsung heroes - the essential tools that turn a mere gathering into an unforgettable soirée.

Bar Essentials: Unveiling the Magic Behind the Bar

Shakers that Rattle the Soul: The heartbeat of any mixologists arsenal, the shaker, is your ticket to libation liberation. Feel the rhythm as you combine spirits and elixirs, transcending the ordinary into the extraordinary.

Muddlers - The Mischief Makers: Embrace the muddle, my friends, for it is the gateway to flavor nirvana. From fresh herbs to succulent fruits, the muddler weaves botanical symphonies, transforming your concoctions into liquid poetry.

Strainers - Sifters of Ambrosia: When your elixir has mingled with the essence of botanical wonders, the strainer steps in. Its the curator, separating the nectar from the earthly remnants, ensuring every sip is pure transcendence.

Jiggers - The Architects of Precision: In the realm of mixology, precision is paramount. The jigger, a maestro of measurements, ensures your libations are an exact dance of spirits, elevating your craft from chaos to composition.

Bar Spoons - Stirring Elegance: A simple yet elegant companion, the bar spoon takes you beyond the shake. With a graceful stir, it marries the flavors, coaxing out subtleties that elevate your concoctions into liquid artistry.

Tips on Wielding the Tools of Libation

Shaking vs. Stirring - The Dance of Texture: When to shake and when to stir is a nuanced decision. Shaking introduces vigor, creating a frothy embrace, while stirring maintains a dignified composure, allowing the spirits to whisper their secrets in harmony.

The Art of Muddling - Bruising with Purpose: Muddling is not a chaotic bash; it's a gentle persuasion. Apply just enough pressure to extract the essence, avoiding a bitter symphony while coaxing the botanicals to dance in your glass.

Straining with Finesse: As you employ the strainer, don't rush the separation. Let gravity work its magic, allowing the liquid gems to cascade into the awaiting vessel. Patience in this step ensures a seamless flow from shaker to glass.

Jigger Mastery - The Goldilocks Principle: Precision is the soul of mixology. Use the jigger as your compass, ensuring each measure is not too much, not too little - just perfect. It's the secret handshake that grants you entry into the realm of cocktail wizardry.

Bar Spoon Serenity: Stirring with a bar spoon is an art of zen. Embrace the circular motion, allowing the spoon to glide effortlessly through the concoction. The result? A libation that bears the signature of your elegant craftsmanship.

As you embark on this mixological journey, consider these tools not just as utensils but as extensions of your creative spirit. Let the spirits flow, the tools dance, and the libations tell tales of flavor and finesse. Here's to crafting the perfect cocktails - may your shakers echo with applause, and your creations linger on palates like a fond memory. Cheers!

Flavor Pairing Suggestions

Ah, so you've delved into the intoxicating realm of 'Quick & Easy Mixology,' where the elixir of life takes shape, one perfectly crafted cocktail at a time. But what's a voyage without a bit of uncharted territory? Enter the Flavor Pairing Suggestions - your compass for navigating the unexplored landscapes of taste.

Think of this section as the backstage pass to mixological brilliance, where we're not just handing you a script but encouraging you to ad-lib, to play with flavors and dance on the edge of the unexpected. This is the jazz of the cocktail world, my friends, and you're the maestro.

Here, amidst the pages of flavor alchemy, you'll find tantalizing whispers of complementary duets and unexpected trios. Like a sommelier pairing wine with a fine meal, we offer you a symphony of suggestions for flavors that not only harmonize but elevate each other to new heights.

Ever considered the sultry dance of citrus and herbs, or the bold tango of spice and sweetness? This is where you shed the constraints of recipes and become the creator, the visionary behind the bar. We're not just giving you fish; we're handing you a net and guiding you to the open sea of mixological possibilities.

As you peruse these flavor pairings, let your imagination take the lead. Infuse your concoctions with the spirit of experimentation, and who knows, you might just stumble upon the next iconic libation. This is the playground where classic meets contemporary, where tradition nods to innovation.

So, my fellow cocktail enthusiast, don't just read; sip, swirl, and savor the inspiration. Let these pairings be the launchpad for your mixological escapades, and may your creations be as unforgettable as the first sip of a perfectly crafted cocktail. Cheers to the art of flavor, the dance of ingredients, and the boundless possibilities that await your ingenious palate.

Table of content

Chapter 1: Classic Elegance

1 glass

5 minutes

Old Fashioned

Ingredients:

- 2 oz bourbon
- 1 sugar cube
- 2-3 dashes Angostura bitters
- Orange twist for garnish

Timeless Elegance: The Old Fashioned
Step back in time with this iconic cocktail. Originating in the 19th century, the Old Fashioned is a classic that has stood the test of time. A symphony of bourbon, sugar, and bitters, it's a drink that whispers tales of sophistication and refinement. Let the amber elixir take you on a journey to the golden era of cocktails.

Directions

1. In a glass, muddle the sugar cube with a splash of water.
2. Add ice cubes and pour bourbon over the sugar.
3. Add bitters and stir well.
4. Garnish with an orange twist.
5. Sip and savor the timeless elegance.

Substitutions

- Try different bitters for a unique twist

1 glass

5 minutes

Normal

Martini

Ingredients:

- 2 oz gin or vodka
- 1/2 oz dry vermouth
- Lemon twist or olive for garnish

Elegance in a Glass: The Perfect Martini
The Martini, a libation of sophistication and mystique. Its origins may be debated, but its impact on cocktail culture is undeniable. With a mix of gin or vodka and a whisper of vermouth, it's a balance of simplicity and complexity. Stir or shake, it's your choice, but every sip is an ode to elegance. Here's to the classic Martini, the epitome of refined taste.

Directions

1. In a mixing glass, combine gin or vodka and vermouth.
2. Fill the glass with ice and stir for 30 seconds.
3. Strain into a chilled martini glass.
4. Garnish with a lemon twist or olive.
5. Cheers to refined taste.

Substitutions

- Experiment with gin and vodka ratios
- Use orange bitters for added depth

1 glass

5 minutes

Negroni

Ingredients:

- 1 oz gin
- 1 oz sweet vermouth
- 1 oz Campari
- Orange slice or twist for garnish

Italian Elegance: The Negroni
Inspired by the vibrant streets of Florence, the Negroni is a celebration of Italian craftsmanship. A balance of gin, vermouth, and Campari, it's a symphony of flavors that dance on your palate. Legend has it, Count Camillo Negroni sparked this creation, forever leaving a mark on the cocktail world. Immerse yourself in the rich heritage of the Negroni.

Directions

1. Fill a mixing glass with ice and add gin, vermouth, and Campari.
2. Stir well to chill the mixture.
3. Strain into a glass over ice.
4. Garnish with an orange slice or twist.
5. Salute to Italian elegance.

Substitutions

- Adjust ratios to suit personal taste
- Try with different gins and vermouths

1 glass

5 minutes

Easy

Whiskey Sour

Citrus Symphony: The Whiskey Sour
The Whiskey Sour, a timeless concoction that marries the robustness of whiskey with the freshness of citrus. Its roots trace back to the mid-19th century, and yet, it remains a favorite on the cocktail scene. With the perfect balance of sweet, sour, and spirit, it's a sip of pure harmony. Raise a glass to the Whiskey Sour, a classic that never goes out of style.

Ingredients:

- 2 oz bourbon
- 3/4 oz fresh lemon juice
- 1/2 oz simple syrup
- Lemon wheel for garnish

Directions

1. In a shaker, combine bourbon, fresh lemon juice, and simple syrup.
2. Add ice and shake well.
3. Strain into a rocks glass over ice.
4. Garnish with a lemon wheel.
5. Enjoy the citrus symphony.

Substitutions

- Use egg white for a frothier texture
- Adjust simple syrup to taste

1 glass

5
minutes

Moscow Mule

Ingredients:

- 2 oz vodka
- 3 oz ginger beer
- 1/2 oz fresh lime juice
- Lime wedge for garnish

Refreshing Classic: The Moscow Mule
Crafted in the 1940s, the Moscow Mule is a refreshing classic that has stood the test of time. A blend of vodka, ginger beer, and lime, served in a copper mug, it's more than a drink–it's an experience. Legend has it, this cocktail was born in the mix of a meeting between a vodka distributor and a ginger beer producer. Sip on the cool, effervescent charm of the Moscow Mule.

Directions

1. Fill a copper mug with ice.
2. Pour vodka and lime juice over the ice.
3. Top with ginger beer and stir gently.
4. Garnish with a lime wedge.
5. Experience the cool effervescence.

Substitutions

- Use flavored ginger beer for a twist
- Add a splash of cranberry juice for a variation

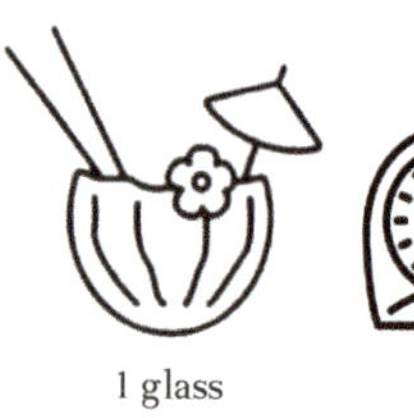

1 glass 10 minutes

Margarita

Ingredients:

2 oz tequila
1 oz triple sec
1 oz fresh lime juice
Salt for rimming the glass

Origins & Popularity: The Margarita, a timeless concoction born from the golden sands of Acapulco, has become a global sensation. Picture yourself seaside, with the salty breeze on your face and a tangy Margarita in hand. Its origins are as vibrant as the drink itself, said to be inspired by a showgirl named Marjorie King, who was allergic to all alcohols except tequila. The Margarita was crafted just for her, and the rest is history. A zesty blend of tequila, triple sec, and fresh lime juice, this cocktail is an ode to the Mexican sun.

Directions

1. Rim a glass with salt.
2. In a shaker, combine tequila, triple sec, and fresh lime juice.
3. Shake well with ice.
4. Strain into the prepared glass.
5. Garnish with a lime wheel.
6. Transport yourself to the shores of Acapulco with each sip.
7. Savor the tangy and zesty flavors.
8. Feel the warmth of the Mexican sun.
9. Cheers to the timeless Margarita.
10. Enjoy the classic cocktail that captures the spirit of the beachside.

Substitutions

-

1 glass

8 minutes

Tom Collins

Ingredients:

2 oz gin
3/4 oz simple syrup
1 oz fresh lemon juice
Soda water
Lemon twist for garnish

Origins & Popularity: The Tom Collins, a sparkling icon in the world of cocktails, traces its roots to the bustling streets of London in the 19th century. It's rumored to be named after the infamous prank of sending unsuspecting folks on a quest for a non-existent character named Tom Collins. Picture this: the sun setting over the River Thames, and you, sipping on a Tom Collins. A symphony of gin, simple syrup, and fresh lemon juice, this effervescent drink is a tribute to the timeless charm of London.

Directions

1. In a shaker, combine gin, simple syrup, and fresh lemon juice.
2. Shake well with ice.
3. Strain into a Collins glass filled with ice.
4. Top with soda water.
5. Stir gently to combine.
6. Garnish with a lemon twist.
7. Imagine the streets of 19th-century London with each sip.
8. Feel the effervescence dance on your palate.
9. Cheers to the classic Tom Collins.
10. Enjoy the sparkling elegance of this timeless cocktail.

Substitutions

-

1 glass

12 minutes

Mojito

Ingredients:

2 oz white rum
1 oz simple syrup
1 oz fresh lime juice
6-8 fresh mint leaves
Soda water
Lime wedge and mint sprig for garnish

Origins & Popularity: The Mojito, a refreshing elixir from the sultry streets of Havana, captures the essence of Cuban cool. Its origins are steeped in history, associated with the 16th-century remedy "El Draque" created by pirate Sir Francis Drake. Picture yourself under the Cuban sun, sipping a Mojito, and dancing to the rhythmic beats of salsa. A fusion of rum, mint, lime, and sugar, this cocktail is a celebration of Caribbean vibrancy.

Directions

1. In a glass, muddle mint leaves with simple syrup and fresh lime juice.
2. Fill the glass with ice.
3. Pour in white rum.
4. Top with soda water.
5. Stir gently.
6. Garnish with a lime wedge and a mint sprig.
7. Transport yourself to the vibrant streets of Havana.
8. Feel the cool breeze of the Caribbean.
9. Cheers to the refreshing Mojito.
10. Enjoy the lively spirit of this Cuban classic.

Substitutions

-

1 glass 8 minutes

Daiquiri

Ingredients:

2 oz white rum
3/4 oz simple syrup
1 oz fresh lime juice

Origins & Popularity: The Daiquiri, a cocktail with humble beginnings in the tropical haven of Santiago de Cuba, has evolved into a global sensation. Its story is entwined with the exploits of an American engineer, Jennings Cox, who concocted this drink in the pursuit of refreshment. Imagine yourself on a sun-drenched Cuban beach, sipping a Daiquiri with the waves at your feet. A perfect blend of rum, simple syrup, and fresh lime juice, this cocktail is a timeless ode to Caribbean elegance.

Directions

1. In a shaker, combine white rum, simple syrup, and fresh lime juice.
2. Shake well with ice.
3. Strain into a chilled coupe glass.
4. Imagine the shores of Santiago de Cuba with each sip.
5. Feel the tropical elegance dance on your palate.
6. Cheers to the classic Daiquiri.
7. Enjoy the timeless allure of this Cuban masterpiece.
8. Let the waves of flavor transport you to the Caribbean.
9. Savor the simplicity of the Daiquiri.
10. Experience the elegance of Caribbean refreshment.

Substitutions

-

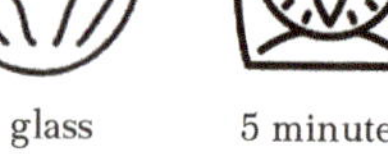

1 glass 5 minutes

Manhattan

Ingredients:

2 oz rye whiskey
1 oz sweet vermouth
2-3 dashes aromatic bitters
Maraschino cherry for garnish

Substitutions

-

Origins & Popularity: The Manhattan, a sophisticated elixir born in the bustling heart of New York City, epitomizes the glamour of the Gilded Age. Its origins are as classic as the city skyline, with tales of its creation at the Manhattan Club in the 1870s. Picture yourself in a dimly lit jazz club, the clinking of glasses, and a smooth jazz melody in the background. A fusion of rye whiskey, sweet vermouth, and aromatic bitters, this cocktail is an homage to the timeless allure of the Big Apple.

Directions

1. In a mixing glass, combine rye whiskey, sweet vermouth, and aromatic bitters.
2. Fill the glass with ice and stir well.
3. Strain into a chilled martini or coupe glass.
4. Garnish with a maraschino cherry.
5. Imagine the glamour of the Gilded Age with each sip.
6. Feel the sophistication envelop your senses.
7. Cheers to the classic Manhattan.
8. Enjoy the timeless allure of this New York masterpiece.
9. Let the jazz notes of flavor transport you to the city that never sleeps.
10. Savor the elegance of the Manhattan.
11. Feel the heartbeat of the Big Apple in every sip.

Chapter 2: Tropical Temptations

1 glass

5 minutes

Piña Colada

Ingredients:

1. 2 oz white rum
2. 3 oz pineapple juice
3. 1 oz coconut cream
4. Pineapple wedge and maraschino cherry for garnish

Escape to the tropics with the Piña Colada, a libation that conjures sandy shores and swaying palms. A blend of coconut, pineapple, and rum, this cocktail is your passport to vacation in a glass.

Directions

1. Fill a blender with ice
2. Add rum, pineapple juice, and coconut cream
3. Blend until smooth
4. Pour into a chilled glass
5. Garnish with a pineapple wedge and maraschino cherry

Substitutions

-

1 glass

7 minutes

Mai Tai

The Mai Tai, a concoction of Polynesian allure, is a balanced blend of light and dark rum, citrusy notes, and almond syrup. A sip will transport you to the golden age of tiki.

Ingredients:

1. 1 1/2 oz light rum
2. 1 1/2 oz dark rum
3. 3/4 oz lime juice
4. 1/2 oz orange liqueur
5. 1/2 oz orgeat syrup
6. Orange twist for garnish

Directions

1. Fill a shaker with ice
2. Add light rum, dark rum, lime juice, orange liqueur, and orgeat syrup
3. Shake well
4. Strain into a rocks glass filled with ice
5. Garnish with an orange twist

Substitutions

-

Sex on the Beach

Ingredients:

1. 1 1/2 oz vodka
2. 1/2 oz peach schnapps
3. 2 oz cranberry juice
4. 2 oz orange juice
5. Orange slice and maraschino cherry for garnish

Indulge in the playful and vibrant Sex on the Beach, a fruity medley of vodka, peach schnapps, and cranberry and orange juices. Each sip is a flirtatious dance of flavors.

Directions

1. Fill a shaker with ice
2. Add vodka, peach schnapps, cranberry juice, and orange juice
3. Shake well
4. Strain into a highball glass filled with ice
5. Garnish with an orange slice and maraschino cherry

Substitutions

-

1 glass

8 minutes

Normal

Bahama Mama

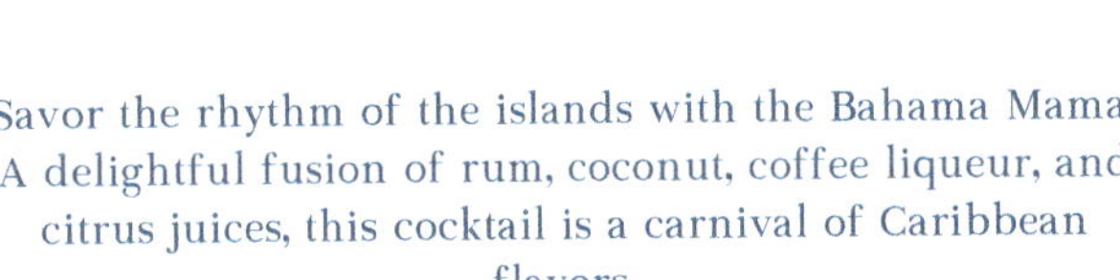

Savor the rhythm of the islands with the Bahama Mama. A delightful fusion of rum, coconut, coffee liqueur, and citrus juices, this cocktail is a carnival of Caribbean flavors.

Ingredients:

1. 1 oz rum
2. 1 oz coconut rum
3. 1/2 oz coffee liqueur
4. 2 oz pineapple juice
5. 1 oz orange juice
6. 1/2 oz grenadine
7. Orange slice and cherry for garnish

Directions

1. Fill a shaker with ice
2. Add rum, coconut rum, coffee liqueur, pineapple juice, orange juice, and grenadine
3. Shake well
4. Strain into a hurricane glass filled with ice
5. Garnish with an orange slice and cherry

Substitutions

-

1 glass

10
minutes

Hurricane

Ingredients:

1. 2 oz dark rum
2. 2 oz light rum
3. 1 oz passion fruit juice
4. 3/4 oz orange juice
5. 1/4 oz grenadine
6. Orange slice and cherry for garnish

Let the Hurricane sweep you off your feet with its bold mix of dark and light rum, passion fruit, and citrus. Crafted for a storm of flavor, it's a libation to weather any occasion.

Directions

1. Fill a shaker with ice
2. Add dark rum, light rum, passion fruit juice, orange juice, and grenadine
3. Shake well
4. Strain into a hurricane glass filled with ice
5. Garnish with an orange slice and cherry

Substitutions

-

1 glass

10 minutes

Easy

Blue Hawaiian

Ingredients:

- 2 oz light rum
- 1 oz blue curaçao
- 2 oz pineapple juice
- 1 oz cream of coconut
- Pineapple slice for garnish
- Ice cubes

Transport yourself to the sandy shores of Hawaii with the iconic Blue Hawaiian. This tropical elixir, adorned with the colors of the ocean, gained fame in the tiki cocktail revolution. A symphony of rum, coconut, and pineapple, it's a sip of paradise in every glass.

Directions

1. Fill a shaker with ice.
2. Add light rum, blue curaçao, pineapple juice, and cream of coconut.
3. Shake well until chilled.
4. Strain into a glass filled with ice.
5. Garnish with a pineapple slice.
6. Sip, and let the waves of flavor roll in.

Substitutions

- Substitute light rum with coconut rum for an extra tropical twist.
- Adjust blue curaçao for desired vibrancy.

1 glass

15 minutes

Normal

Mango Tango

Ingredients:

- 2 oz mango rum
- 1 oz fresh mango puree
- 1 oz lime juice
- 1 oz simple syrup
- Fresh mint leaves for garnish
- Ice cubes

Get ready for a dance of flavors with the Mango Tango. Born in the vibrant streets of Havana, this cocktail is a celebration of juicy mangoes and the rhythm of Cuban beats. Shake, shimmy, and sip your way to a tropical escapade in every refreshing gulp.

Directions

1. In a shaker, muddle fresh mint leaves.
2. Add mango rum, mango puree, lime juice, and simple syrup.
3. Shake vigorously.
4. Strain into a glass filled with ice.
5. Garnish with mint leaves.
6. Take a sip and let the mango tango unfold.

Substitutions

- Use mango nectar if fresh mango is unavailable.
- Experiment with flavored rum for a unique twist.

1 glass

12 minutes

Coconut Mojito

Break away from tradition with the Coconut Mojito—a Caribbean-inspired concoction. Originating from the breezy beaches of Puerto Rico, this mojito adds a creamy twist with coconut. It's a refreshing blend of mint, lime, and coconut, inviting you to unwind in style.

Ingredients:

- 2 oz coconut rum
- 1 oz coconut cream
- 1 oz fresh lime juice
- 1 tsp sugar
- Fresh mint leaves for garnish
- Soda water
- Ice cubes

Directions

1. In a glass, muddle mint leaves, lime juice, and sugar.
2. Fill the glass with ice.
3. Pour coconut rum and coconut cream.
4. Top with soda water.
5. Stir gently.
6. Garnish with mint leaves.
7. Sip and let the tropical breeze carry you away.

Substitutions

- Substitute coconut cream with coconut milk for a lighter version.
- Try agave syrup as a sugar alternative.

1 glass

8 minutes

Passion Fruit Caipirinha

From the bustling streets of Brazil comes the Passion Fruit Caipirinha—a zesty twist to the classic. Crafted with the Brazilian spirit, it's a carnival of flavors. The boldness of cachaça meets the tropical allure of passion fruit, creating a cocktail that's a fiesta in every sip.

Ingredients:

- 2 oz cachaça
- 1 passion fruit, halved
- 1 tbsp sugar
- Ice cubes

Directions

1. Scoop the passion fruit into a glass.
2. Add sugar and muddle to extract the juice.
3. Fill the glass with ice.
4. Pour cachaça over the ice.
5. Stir gently.
6. Raise your glass to the rhythm of Brazil.

Substitutions

- Swap passion fruit with any other tropical fruit.
- Adjust sugar to your sweetness preference.

1 glass

10 minutes

Guava Margarita

Ingredients:

- 2 oz tequila
- 1 oz triple sec
- 2 oz guava juice
- 1 oz fresh lime juice
- Salt for rimming
- Lime wedge for garnish
- Ice cubes

Let the fiesta begin with the Guava Margarita—a Mexican twist on a classic favorite. This vibrant cocktail, born in the heart of Jalisco, marries the tanginess of guava with the kick of tequila. A fiesty blend that promises a lively party in every sip.

Directions

1. Rim the glass with salt.
2. Fill the glass with ice.
3. In a shaker, combine tequila, triple sec, guava juice, and lime juice.
4. Shake well.
5. Strain into the prepared glass.
6. Garnish with a lime wedge.
7. Savor the fiesta in a glass.

Substitutions

- Experiment with different fruit juices for a fruity twist.
- Adjust tequila for your preferred strength.

Chapter 3: Fruity Fusion

1 glass

10 minutes

Berry Bliss Smash

Unleash a symphony of berries in this refreshing concoction. Originating from sun-soaked orchards, this smash became a legend in garden gatherings.
A burst of berries awaits with a hint of mint to elevate your spirits.

Ingredients:

- 1 cup mixed berries (strawberries, blueberries, raspberries)
- 2 oz gin
- 1 oz simple syrup
- 1 oz fresh lemon juice
- 5-6 fresh mint leaves
- Ice cubes

Directions

1. In a shaker, muddle mixed berries and mint leaves.
2. Add gin, simple syrup, and lemon juice.
3. Shake well.
4. Strain into a glass filled with ice.
5. Garnish with a mint sprig.

Substitutions

- Blueberries for mixed berries

1 glass

8 minutes

Watermelon Basil Refresher

Dive into summer with this vibrant refresher. Hailing from Mediterranean shores, it's a dance of watermelon sweetness and basil's herbal notes.
Sip, and let the waves of refreshment carry you away.

Ingredients:

- 2 cups fresh watermelon chunks
- 4-5 fresh basil leaves
- 1 oz vodka
- 1 oz simple syrup
- 1 oz lime juice
- Ice cubes

Directions

1. In a blender, combine watermelon and basil.
2. Strain the juice.
3. In a shaker, mix watermelon-basil juice, vodka, simple syrup, and lime juice.
4. Shake well.
5. Pour over ice.

Substitutions

- Mint leaves for basil

1 glass

5 minutes

Cucumber Mint Cooler

A garden-fresh elixir that whispers cool breezes. Born from a love affair with cucumbers and mint, it's the perfect antidote to a scorching day.
Sip slowly and let the crispness rejuvenate your soul.

Ingredients:

- 1/2 cucumber, sliced
- 6-8 fresh mint leaves
- 2 oz gin
- 1 oz simple syrup
- 1 oz lime juice
- Soda water
- Ice cubes

Directions

1. In a glass, muddle cucumber slices and mint leaves.
2. Add gin, simple syrup, and lime juice.
3. Top with ice and fill with soda water.
4. Stir gently.
5. Garnish with a cucumber wheel.

Substitutions

- Elderflower syrup for simple syrup

1 glass

12 minutes

Pineapple Sage Sparkler

Ingredients:

- 1 cup fresh pineapple chunks
- 4-5 fresh sage leaves
- 2 oz white rum
- 1 oz coconut cream
- 1 oz lime juice
- Sparkling water
- Ice cubes

Embark on a tropical journey with this effervescent sparkler. Pineapple and sage collide, creating a sip of paradise.
Let the bubbles carry you away on a wave of fruity delight.

Directions

1. In a blender, blend pineapple and sage until smooth.
2. In a shaker, mix pineapple-sage puree, white rum, coconut cream, and lime juice.
3. Shake well.
4. Strain into a glass with ice.
5. Top with sparkling water.

Substitutions

- Coconut milk for coconut cream

1 glass

7 minutes

Grapefruit Rosemary Fizz

A symphony of tangy grapefruit and aromatic rosemary, this fizz is a salute to citrus lovers.
Refreshment with a twist, perfect for lazy afternoons or lively gatherings.

Ingredients:

- 1 cup fresh grapefruit juice
- 2 oz vodka
- 1 oz honey syrup (equal parts honey and hot water)
- 1 sprig fresh rosemary
- Soda water
- Ice cubes

Directions

1. In a shaker, mix grapefruit juice, vodka, and honey syrup.
2. Add a sprig of rosemary and shake well.
3. Strain into a glass filled with ice.
4. Top with soda water.
5. Garnish with a rosemary sprig.

Substitutions

- Agave syrup for honey syrup

1 glass

5 minutes

Easy

Kiwi Strawberry Sling

Ingredients:

- 2 oz kiwi-infused vodka
- 4 fresh strawberries, hulled and sliced
- 1 oz simple syrup
- 1 oz fresh lime juice
- Soda water
- Kiwi slice and strawberry for garnish

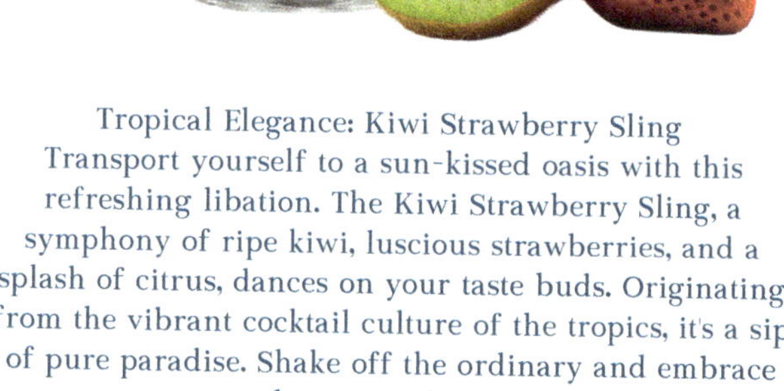

Tropical Elegance: Kiwi Strawberry Sling
Transport yourself to a sun-kissed oasis with this refreshing libation. The Kiwi Strawberry Sling, a symphony of ripe kiwi, luscious strawberries, and a splash of citrus, dances on your taste buds. Originating from the vibrant cocktail culture of the tropics, it's a sip of pure paradise. Shake off the ordinary and embrace the extraordinary.

Directions

1. In a shaker, muddle strawberries and simple syrup.
2. Add kiwi-infused vodka and lime juice.
3. Shake well and strain into a glass over ice.
4. Top with soda water.
5. Garnish with a kiwi slice and strawberry.
6. Sip and savor the tropical elegance.

Substitutions

- Try different flavored vodkas
- Adjust sweetness with more or less simple syrup

1 glass

5 minutes

Peach Basil Bellini

Ingredients:

- 2 oz peach puree
- Fresh basil leaves
- Prosecco
- Peach slice for garnish

Italian Finesse: Peach Basil Bellini
Inspired by the charming streets of Italy, the Peach Basil Bellini is a celebration of summer sophistication. A blend of ripe peaches, fragrant basil, and bubbly prosecco, it's a toast to la dolce vita. Originating from Harry's Bar in Venice, this cocktail captures the essence of timeless elegance. Raise your glass and revel in the peachy perfection.

Directions

1. In a blender, combine peach puree and a few basil leaves.
2. Blend until smooth.
3. Strain into a chilled flute.
4. Top with prosecco.
5. Garnish with a peach slice.
6. Toast to the sweet life.

Substitutions

- Use frozen peaches for a frosty twist
- Experiment with different herbs

1 glass

7 minutes

Blueberry Lavender Lemonade

Ingredients:

- 1 cup fresh blueberries
- 2 tbsp dried lavender buds
- 1 cup sugar
- 1 cup fresh lemon juice
- Sparkling water
- Fresh lavender sprigs for garnish

Floral Bliss: Blueberry Lavender Lemonade
Indulge in the delicate dance of blueberries and lavender with this enchanting lemonade. Crafted for warm afternoons, it's a melody of sweet, tart, and floral notes. Originating from a secret garden of flavors, it's a sip that transports you to a place where time slows down, and every moment is a celebration of taste. Savor the symphony.

Directions

1. In a saucepan, combine blueberries, lavender buds, and sugar.
2. Simmer until sugar dissolves.
3. Strain the syrup and let it cool.
4. In a glass, combine syrup and fresh lemon juice.
5. Add ice and top with sparkling water.
6. Garnish with lavender sprigs.
7. Immerse yourself in floral bliss.

Substitutions

- Adjust sweetness with more or less syrup
- Add vodka for a spirited version

1 glass 5 minutes

Raspberry Mint Julep

Ingredients:

- 2 oz bourbon
- 1/2 cup fresh raspberries
- Fresh mint leaves
- 1/2 oz simple syrup
- Crushed ice
- Raspberry and mint sprig for garnish

Southern Charm: Raspberry Mint Julep
Elevate the classic Mint Julep with the sweet embrace of raspberries. Originating from the heart of the South, this cocktail marries the timeless charm of bourbon with the vibrancy of fresh raspberries and mint. Sip slowly, savor each moment, and let the Raspberry Mint Julep transport you to a breezy afternoon on a Southern porch.

Directions

1. In a glass, muddle raspberries and mint leaves with simple syrup.
2. Add bourbon and fill the glass with crushed ice.
3. Stir gently.
4. Garnish with a raspberry and mint sprig.
5. Experience Southern charm in a glass.

Substitutions

- Experiment with different berries
- Adjust sweetness to taste

Blackberry Thyme Sparkling Wine

Ingredients:

- 1/2 cup fresh blackberries
- 4 sprigs fresh thyme
- 1 oz honey
- Sparkling wine
- Blackberries and thyme for garnish

Effervescent Delight: Blackberry Thyme Sparkling Wine Raise a glass to effervescence with this elegant creation. The Blackberry Thyme Sparkling Wine, born from a garden of flavors, intertwines the richness of blackberries with the subtle herbal notes of thyme. Whether you're toasting to a special occasion or simply celebrating life, let this sparkling concoction be your companion.

Directions

1. In a shaker, muddle blackberries, thyme, and honey.
2. Strain the mixture into a flute glass.
3. Top with sparkling wine.
4. Garnish with blackberries and thyme.
5. Cheers to effervescent delight.

Substitutions

- Use elderflower liqueur for a floral twist
- Adjust sweetness with more or less honey

Chapter 4: Citrus Sensations

1 glass

8 minutes

Citrus Burst Martini

Ingredients:

2 oz vodka
3/4 oz triple sec
1 oz fresh orange juice
1/2 oz fresh lemon juice
Orange twist for garnish

Substitutions

-

Origins & Popularity: The Citrus Burst Martini, a dazzling creation inspired by the lively streets of New Orleans, is a symphony of citrus flavors that dance on your palate. Imagine the energy of a jazz band echoing through the French Quarter as you sip this cocktail. Crafted to embody the spirit of the city, this martini is a testament to the vibrant cocktail culture that defines New Orleans. A burst of citrusy joy awaits in every sip, a celebration in a glass.

Directions

1. In a shaker, combine vodka, triple sec, fresh orange juice, and fresh lemon juice.
2. Shake well with ice.
3. Strain into a chilled martini glass.
4. Garnish with an orange twist.
5. Imagine the lively streets of New Orleans with each sip.
6. Feel the burst of citrus flavors on your palate.
7. Cheers to the Citrus Burst Martini.
8. Enjoy the lively spirit of this New Orleans-inspired elixir.
9. Let the jazz notes of flavor transport you to the heart of the French Quarter.
10. Savor the celebration in every sip.

1 glass

10 minutes

Orange Blossom Paloma

Ingredients:

2 oz tequila
1 oz fresh grapefruit juice
1/2 oz fresh lime juice
1/2 oz orange blossom honey syrup
Club soda
Grapefruit wedge for garnish

Origins & Popularity: The Orange Blossom Paloma, a refreshing libation inspired by the sun-kissed orchards of Mexico, is a citrusy delight that transports you to the heart of agave country. Picture yourself under the shade of orange blossoms, sipping this Paloma and feeling the warmth of the Mexican sun. Crafted with tequila and a burst of citrus, this cocktail is a tribute to the simplicity and beauty of Mexican flavors. A blossoming journey awaits with every sip.

Directions

1. In a shaker, combine tequila, fresh grapefruit juice, fresh lime juice, and orange blossom honey syrup.
2. Shake well with ice.
3. Strain into a highball glass filled with ice.
4. Top with club soda.
5. Stir gently.
6. Garnish with a grapefruit wedge.
7. Transport yourself to the sun-kissed orchards of Mexico with each sip.
8. Feel the blossom of flavors on your palate.
9. Cheers to the Orange Blossom Paloma.
10. Enjoy the refreshing journey of this Mexican-inspired elixir.
11. Savor the citrusy delight.

Substitutions

-

Lemon Ginger Drop

Ingredients:

2 oz vodka
3/4 oz fresh lemon juice
1/2 oz ginger syrup
Lemon twist and candied ginger for garnish

Origins & Popularity: The Lemon Ginger Drop, a zesty creation that pays homage to the timeless appeal of a lemon drop cocktail with a gingery twist, is a burst of sunshine in every sip. Inspired by the eclectic vibes of a summer garden, this cocktail is as refreshing as a cool breeze on a warm day. Picture yourself surrounded by lemon trees and blooming ginger, and you have the essence of this delightful elixir. A perfect fusion of citrus and spice awaits your palate.

Directions

1. In a shaker, combine vodka, fresh lemon juice, and ginger syrup.
2. Shake well with ice.
3. Strain into a sugar-rimmed martini glass.
4. Garnish with a lemon twist and candied ginger.
5. Imagine the vibrant hues of a summer garden with each sip.
6. Feel the zesty and gingery burst of flavors.
7. Cheers to the Lemon Ginger Drop.
8. Enjoy the refreshing twist on a classic.
9. Let the citrus and spice dance on your palate.
10. Savor the burst of sunshine in every sip.

Substitutions

1 glass

5 minutes

Easy

Grapefruit Elderflower Spritz

Ingredients:

2 oz vodka
1 oz elderflower liqueur
1 oz fresh grapefruit juice
Club soda
Grapefruit twist for garnish

Origins & Popularity: The Grapefruit Elderflower Spritz, a effervescent concoction inspired by the chic cafes of Paris, is a light and floral libation that elevates any moment. Imagine yourself at a sidewalk cafe, the Eiffel Tower in the background, and a crisp spritz in hand. Crafted with the elegance of elderflower and the citrusy zing of grapefruit, this cocktail is a toast to sophistication. With each sip, you'll feel transported to the romantic allure of the City of Light. A refreshing escape awaits.

Directions

1. In a wine glass, combine vodka, elderflower liqueur, and fresh grapefruit juice.
2. Fill the glass with ice.
3. Top with club soda.
4. Stir gently.
5. Garnish with a grapefruit twist.
6. Transport yourself to the chic cafes of Paris with each sip.
7. Feel the elegance and effervescence on your palate.
8. Cheers to the Grapefruit Elderflower Spritz.
9. Enjoy the sophisticated escape.
10. Let the floral notes dance on your taste buds.
11. Savor the romantic allure of this Parisian-inspired elixir.

Substitutions

-

1 glass

8 minutes

Lime Mint Spritzer

Ingredients:

2 oz gin
1 oz fresh lime juice
1/2 oz simple syrup
Club soda
Fresh mint leaves for garnish

Origins & Popularity: The Lime Mint Spritzer, a revitalizing creation inspired by the lively markets of Marrakech, is a citrusy and minty escape that invigorates your senses. Picture yourself in a bustling souk, the aroma of fresh limes and mint in the air. Crafted with the zing of lime and the cooling embrace of mint, this spritzer is a tribute to the vibrant energy of Moroccan bazaars. With each sip, you'll embark on a sensory journey to the heart of Marrakech. Refreshment beckons.

Directions

1. In a highball glass, combine gin, fresh lime juice, and simple syrup.
2. Fill the glass with ice.
3. Top with club soda.
4. Stir gently.
5. Garnish with fresh mint leaves.
6. Picture yourself in the lively markets of Marrakech with each sip.
7. Feel the invigorating citrusy and minty embrace.
8. Cheers to the Lime Mint Spritzer.
9. Enjoy the revitalizing escape.
10. Let the vibrant energy of Moroccan bazaars awaken your senses.
11. Savor the refreshment in every sip.

Substitutions

-

1 glass

10 minutes

Blood Orange Margarita

A sunny twist on the classic, this Blood Orange Margarita brings the warmth of Mexico with the zing of citrus.
Crafted with premium tequila, triple sec, and fresh blood orange juice.

Ingredients:

- 2 oz premium tequila
- 1 oz triple sec
- 1.5 oz fresh blood orange juice
- 0.5 oz lime juice
- 1 oz simple syrup
- Salt for rimming
- Ice

Directions

1. Rim the glass with salt.
2. In a shaker, combine tequila, triple sec, blood orange juice, lime juice, and simple syrup.
3. Shake well with ice.
4. Strain into the rimmed glass over ice.
5. Garnish with a blood orange slice.

Substitutions

-

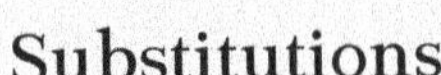

1 glass

8 minutes

Tangerine Basil Smash

The Tangerine Basil Smash is a garden in a glass. Fresh tangerines and fragrant basil dance together, creating a symphony of flavors.
Ideal for a refreshing sip under the sun.

Ingredients:

- 2 oz gin
- 1 oz tangerine juice
- 0.75 oz simple syrup
- 4-6 fresh basil leaves
- Ice

Directions

1. Muddle basil leaves in a shaker.
2. Add gin, tangerine juice, and simple syrup.
3. Shake well with ice.
4. Strain into a glass over fresh ice.
5. Garnish with a sprig of basil and a tangerine wheel.

Substitutions

-

1 glass

12 minutes

Citrus Mint Mojito

Ingredients:

- 2 oz white rum
- 1 oz lime juice
- 0.75 oz simple syrup
- 6-8 fresh mint leaves
- Club soda
- Ice

Transport yourself to the lively streets of Havana with the Citrus Mint Mojito. This Cuban classic gets a zesty makeover with a citrus twist and a hint of refreshing mint.

Directions

1. Muddle mint leaves with lime juice and simple syrup in a glass.
2. Fill the glass with ice.
3. Pour rum over the ice.
4. Top with club soda.
5. Stir gently and garnish with a mint sprig.

-

1 glass

15 minutes

Normal

Kumquat Cucumber Collins

Ingredients:

- 2 oz gin
- 1 oz kumquat syrup
- 0.75 oz lemon juice
- 4-6 cucumber slices
- Club soda
- Ice

An effervescent elixir, the Kumquat Cucumber Collins is a garden-inspired cocktail that marries the sweetness of kumquats with the crispness of cucumber. A true summer delight.

Directions

1. In a shaker, muddle cucumber slices.
2. Add gin, kumquat syrup, and lemon juice.
3. Shake well with ice.
4. Strain into a glass over ice.
5. Top with club soda and stir gently.
6. Garnish with a kumquat slice and cucumber ribbon.

Substitutions

-

1 glass

8 minutes

Yuzu Sake Sour

Ingredients:

- 2 oz sake
- 1 oz yuzu juice
- 0.75 oz simple syrup
- 1 egg white
- Ice

Take a journey to the Far East with the Yuzu Sake Sour. The Japanese citrus, yuzu, adds a tangy twist to the traditional sour, complemented by the smoothness of sake.
Elegant and enticing.

Directions

1. In a shaker, combine sake, yuzu juice, simple syrup, and egg white.
2. Shake vigorously without ice to emulsify the egg white.
3. Add ice and shake again.
4. Strain into a glass.
5. Garnish with a twist of yuzu peel.

Substitutions

-

Chapter 5: Herbal Infusions

1 glass

10 minutes

Basil Grapefruit Fizz

Let's dive into the vibrant world of the Basil Grapefruit Fizz. This effervescent delight emerged from the sun-soaked streets of Italy, where basil and grapefruit found a harmonious partnership. It's a dance of freshness and zest that will transport you to a breezy Italian terrace with every sip. Salute!

Ingredients:

- 2 oz gin
- 1 oz fresh grapefruit juice
- 0.5 oz simple syrup
- 3-4 fresh basil leaves
- Soda water
- Grapefruit twist for garnish
- Ice cubes

Directions

1. In a shaker, muddle basil leaves with simple syrup.
2. Add gin and grapefruit juice.
3. Shake well.
4. Strain into a glass filled with ice.
5. Top with soda water.
6. Garnish with a grapefruit twist.
7. Sip and let the basil and grapefruit duet enchant your senses.

Substitutions

- Swap gin for vodka for a milder flavor.
- Try lemon juice if grapefruits are out of season.

1 glass

12 minutes

Rosemary Maple Bourbon

Ingredients:

- 2 oz bourbon
- 0.75 oz pure maple syrup
- 0.5 oz fresh lemon juice
- 1 sprig of rosemary
- Orange twist for garnish
- Ice cubes

Picture yourself in a cozy cabin, nestled in the woods, as you savor the Rosemary Maple Bourbon. Born from the rustic charm of American distilleries, this cocktail marries the robust notes of bourbon with the earthy sweetness of maple. A fireside companion that brings warmth and sophistication to your glass.

Directions

1. In a shaker, combine bourbon, maple syrup, and lemon juice.
2. Shake well.
3. Strip rosemary leaves from the sprig and add to the shaker.
4. Shake again to infuse the flavors.
5. Strain into a glass with ice.
6. Garnish with an orange twist.
7. Sip slowly, savoring the rustic charm of rosemary and maple.

Substitutions

- Experiment with different whiskey varieties.
- Substitute rosemary with thyme for a subtle twist.

1 glass

8 minutes

Thyme Honey Bee's Knees

The Thyme Honey Bee's Knees is a tribute to the golden age of cocktails. Originating from the speakeasies of the 1920s, this concoction balances the sweet allure of honey with the herbal touch of thyme. It's a time-traveling elixir that whispers tales of jazz, flapper dresses, and clandestine celebrations.

Ingredients:

- 2 oz gin
- 0.75 oz honey syrup (1:1 honey and water)
- 0.75 oz fresh lemon juice
- 3-4 sprigs of fresh thyme
- Lemon twist for garnish
- Ice cubes

Directions

1. In a shaker, combine gin, honey syrup, and lemon juice.
2. Add thyme sprigs to the shaker.
3. Shake well to release thyme essence.
4. Strain into a glass filled with ice.
5. Garnish with a lemon twist.
6. Inhale the aromas, take a sip, and transport yourself to the roaring twenties.

Substitutions

- Use flavored honey for a unique twist.
- Swap thyme with basil for a different herbal note.

1 glass

15 minutes

Sage and Blackberry Smash

Ingredients:

- 2 oz gin
- 1 oz blackberry syrup
- 0.5 oz fresh lime juice
- 5-6 fresh sage leaves
- Blackberries for garnish
- Ice cubes

In the garden of mixology, the Sage and Blackberry Smash stands tall as a masterpiece. Inspired by the hedgerows of England, this cocktail marries the boldness of blackberries with the savory grace of sage. It's a journey through the English countryside in a glass, where berries and herbs dance in delightful harmony.

Directions

1. In a shaker, muddle sage leaves with blackberry syrup.
2. Add gin and lime juice.
3. Shake well.
4. Strain into a glass filled with ice.
5. Garnish with fresh blackberries.
6. Sip slowly, letting the symphony of sage and blackberry unfold on your palate.

Substitutions

- Experiment with different berries for a burst of flavors.
- Infuse the syrup with rosemary for an herbal twist.

1 glass

10 minutes

Easy

Lavender Gin Tonic

Ingredients:

- 2 oz lavender-infused gin
- 0.75 oz lavender syrup
- 0.5 oz fresh lime juice
- Tonic water
- Lavender sprig for garnish
- Ice cubes

Embark on a sensory journey with the Lavender Gin Tonic. Inspired by the fields of Provence, this cocktail is a delicate dance of floral notes and effervescence. The lavender-infused gin transforms a classic into a fragrant masterpiece. It's a sip of southern France, where every bubble carries the essence of lavender fields.

Directions

1. In a glass, combine lavender-infused gin, lavender syrup, and lime juice.
2. Fill the glass with ice.
3. Top with tonic water.
4. Stir gently to mix.
5. Garnish with a lavender sprig.
6. Sip and let the fragrance of lavender transport you to the sun-soaked fields of Provence.

Substitutions

- Make a non-alcoholic version with lavender-infused lemonade.
- Adjust the sweetness by varying the amount of lavender syrup.

1 glass

15 minutes

Minted Pineapple Rum Punch

Ingredients:

- 1 cup fresh pineapple chunks
- 2 oz dark rum
- 1 oz fresh lime juice
- 0.5 oz simple syrup
- 8-10 fresh mint leaves
- Ice cubes

Sail away to the tropics with this zesty elixir. Born in the Caribbean, this punch marries the sweetness of pineapple with the kick of mint and rum. A vacation in a glass.

Directions

1. Muddle pineapple and mint in a shaker.
2. Add dark rum, lime juice, and simple syrup.
3. Shake well.
4. Strain into a glass filled with ice.
5. Garnish with a mint sprig.
6. Sip and set sail on a journey of flavors.

Substitutions

- Light rum for dark rum

1glass 12 minutes

Cilantro Jalapeño Margarita

Ingredients:

- 2 oz tequila
- 1 oz triple sec
- 1 oz fresh lime juice
- 1/2 oz agave syrup
- 3-4 slices jalapeño
- Fresh cilantro
- Salt for rimming
- Ice cubes

Spice up your fiesta with this margarita that dances on the edge of bold and refreshing. Originating from lively Mexican streets, it's a kick of cilantro and jalapeño in every sip.
The party starter.

Directions

1. In a shaker, muddle cilantro and jalapeño.
2. Add tequila, triple sec, lime juice, and agave syrup.
3. Shake well.
4. Rim the glass with salt.
5. Strain the mixture into the glass over ice.
6. Garnish with cilantro.
7. Sip and let the fiesta begin.

Substitutions

- Honey for agave syrup

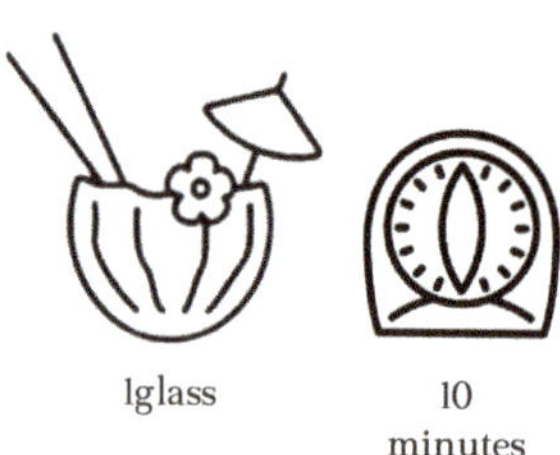

Lemongrass Ginger Sparkler

Ingredients:

- 1 stalk lemongrass, sliced
- 1-inch ginger, sliced
- 2 oz vodka
- 1 oz honey syrup (equal parts honey and hot water)
- Soda water
- Ice cubes

Experience the harmony of lemongrass and ginger in this bubbly sensation. Crafted in Southeast Asia, it's a symphony of flavors that will tingle your taste buds. Refreshment elevated.

Directions

1. In a glass, muddle lemongrass and ginger.
2. Add vodka and honey syrup.
3. Fill the glass with ice.
4. Top with soda water.
5. Stir gently.
6. Sip and let the exotic flavors transport you.

Substitutions

- Simple syrup for honey syrup

1glass

8 minutes

Chamomile Citrus Tea Cocktail

Ingredients:

- 1 chamomile tea bag
- 1 oz gin
- 1 oz orange liqueur
- 1 oz fresh lemon juice
- 0.5 oz simple syrup
- Lemon twist for garnish
- Ice cubes

A calming elixir with a citrus twist. Inspired by English gardens, this cocktail combines the tranquility of chamomile tea with the zest of citrus. Sip and let the stress melt away.

Directions

1. Brew chamomile tea and let it cool.
2. In a shaker, mix tea, gin, orange liqueur, lemon juice, and simple syrup.
3. Shake well.
4. Strain into a glass with ice.
5. Garnish with a lemon twist.
6. Sip and find your peaceful moment.

Substitutions

- Grand Marnier for orange liqueur

lglass

7 minutes

Dill Cucumber Vodka Cooler

Crisp and invigorating, this cooler is a salute to summertime. With dill and cucumber, it's a garden party in a glass.
Cool down and revel in the freshness.

Ingredients:

- 4 slices cucumber
- 2 sprigs fresh dill
- 2 oz vodka
- 1 oz elderflower liqueur
- 1 oz fresh lime juice
- Soda water
- Ice cubes

Directions

1. In a glass, muddle cucumber slices and dill.
2. Add vodka, elderflower liqueur, and lime juice.
3. Fill the glass with ice.
4. Top with soda water.
5. Stir gently.
6. Sip and let the cool breeze of flavors envelop you.

Substitutions

- St. Germain for elderflower liqueur

We have a small favor to ask

Amidst the swirling symphony of spirits and the clinking of ice, youve delved into the realm of libation creation with Quick & Easy Mixology. As we traverse the landscape of cocktails together, lets take a brief detour - not into the world of garnishes and shakers, but into the digital expanse where your thoughts become the garnish for our humble concoctions.

Reviews, my fellow mixologists, are the elusive nectar of our craft. In the realm of small publishers like ours, theyre as rare as a perfectly shaken martini. So, heres the deal: if youve found yourself shaking and stirring joyfully through our pages, if the recipes have tickled your taste buds and elevated your spirits, I implore you to be our guide.

Now, I get it. Were all busy crafting, sipping, and enjoying lifes spirited moments. But if you can carve out a moment, head back to the digital bazaar where you acquired this liquid treasure trove. Seek out that mystical review button - its not just a button; its the cocktail shaker of the digital realm.

A rating, a few words - a gesture that might seem as fleeting as the aroma of a freshly muddled herb, but in our world, its the aromatic note that lingers, defining the essence of our concoctions.

In the kingdom of mixology, your review is the secret ingredient that weaves through the recipes, offering fellow imbibers a glimpse into the alchemy that transpires when spirits and creativity collide. Its not just a review; its the cocktail party chatter, the shared enthusiasm for the art of mixing.

As we navigate this spirited journey together, know that every review is a sip of encouragement we savor. We appreciate and relish each one, recognizing the effort it takes to pen down your thoughts amidst the clinking of glasses.

And if, perchance, you spot a minor hiccup or a subtle discord in our liquid symphony, rest assured, weve toiled over the bar, aiming for the perfect pour. Mistakes, like a dash too much or too little, can happen, and we hope youll join us in toasting to the imperfections that make our mixology adventure uniquely ours.

Now, lets return to the heart of the matter - the recipes. Stir, shake, and pour with the zeal of a seasoned mixologist. Your journey through these pages is not just a solo expedition; its a communal toast to the joy of crafting the perfect cocktail.

In closing, I raise my metaphorical glass to you, fellow aficionado of libations. Your review, my friends, is the zest that elevates our spirits and keeps the cocktail shaker of creativity shaking. May your drinks be bold, your garnishes be plentiful, and your reviews be as effervescent as the bubbles in a freshly popped bottle of champagne. Cheers!

Chapter 6: Spicy Delights

1 glass 8 minutes

Spicy Mango Jalapeño Margarita

Ingredients:

- 2 oz silver tequila
- 1 oz triple sec
- 2 oz fresh mango puree
- 1 oz fresh lime juice
- Jalapeño slices
- Tajin for rimming
- Mango slice and jalapeño for garnish

Exotic Heat: Spicy Mango Jalapeño Margarita
Embark on a journey of bold flavors with this spicy libation. The Spicy Mango Jalapeño Margarita is a fusion of tropical sweetness, fiery jalapeño, and the smooth embrace of tequila. Originating from the bustling streets of Mexico, it's a celebration of zest and heat. Sip slowly, let the warmth linger, and relish the dance of flavors.

Directions

1. Rim the glass with Tajin.
2. In a shaker, muddle jalapeño slices.
3. Add tequila, triple sec, mango puree, and lime juice.
4. Shake well and strain into the glass.
5. Garnish with mango slice and jalapeño.
6. Savor the exotic heat.

Substitutions

- Adjust spiciness by controlling jalapeño seeds
- Use agave syrup for added sweetness

1 glass

6 minutes

Easy

Jalapeño Pineapple Moscow Mule

Ingredients:

- 2 oz vodka
- 3 oz pineapple juice
- 1 oz fresh lime juice
- Ginger beer
- Jalapeño slices
- Pineapple wedge for garnish

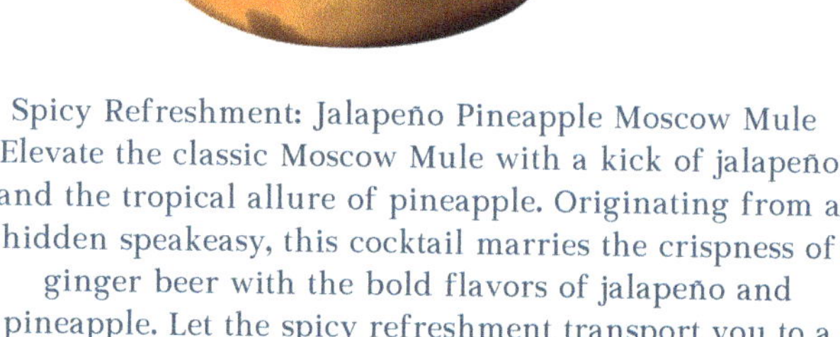

Spicy Refreshment: Jalapeño Pineapple Moscow Mule
Elevate the classic Moscow Mule with a kick of jalapeño and the tropical allure of pineapple. Originating from a hidden speakeasy, this cocktail marries the crispness of ginger beer with the bold flavors of jalapeño and pineapple. Let the spicy refreshment transport you to a world where every sip is an adventure.

Directions

1. In a copper mug, muddle jalapeño slices.
2. Add vodka, pineapple juice, and lime juice.
3. Fill the mug with ice.
4. Top with ginger beer.
5. Stir gently and garnish with a pineapple wedge.
6. Enjoy the spicy refreshment.

Substitutions

- Experiment with different flavored vodkas
- Adjust sweetness with more or less pineapple juice

1 glass

7 minutes

Habanero Passion Fruit Martini

Ingredients:

- 2 oz vodka
- 1 oz habanero-infused simple syrup
- 2 oz passion fruit puree
- 1 oz lime juice
- Passion fruit seeds for garnish

Fiery Elegance: Habanero Passion Fruit Martini
Indulge in the daring elegance of the Habanero Passion Fruit Martini. This fiery creation, inspired by the sultry nights of the Caribbean, combines the heat of habanero with the exotic sweetness of passion fruit. Originating from a beachside bar, it's a cocktail that balances intensity with sophistication. Sip slowly and let the heat unfold.

Directions

1. In a shaker, combine vodka, habanero-infused simple syrup, passion fruit puree, and lime juice.
2. Shake well with ice.
3. Strain into a martini glass.
4. Garnish with passion fruit seeds.
5. Embrace the fiery elegance.

Substitutions

- Adjust sweetness with more or less simple syrup
- Infuse vodka with habanero for a stronger kick

1 glass 8 minutes

Sriracha Bloody Mary

Ingredients:

- 2 oz vodka
- 4 oz tomato juice
- 1/2 oz fresh lemon juice
- 1 tsp Worcestershire sauce
- Sriracha to taste
- Celery salt for rimming
- Celery stalk and lemon wedge for garnish

Bold Awakening: Sriracha Bloody Mary
Rise and shine with a bold twist on the classic Bloody Mary. The Sriracha Bloody Mary, inspired by the lively streets of Bangkok, adds a spicy kick to your morning ritual. A harmonious blend of tomatoes, citrus, and Sriracha, it's a wake-up call for your taste buds. Start your day with a bold awakening.

Directions

1. Rim the glass with celery salt.
2. In a shaker, combine vodka, tomato juice, lemon juice, Worcestershire sauce, and Sriracha.
3. Shake well with ice.
4. Strain into the glass.
5. Garnish with a celery stalk and lemon wedge.
6. Cheers to a bold awakening.

Substitutions

- Adjust spiciness with more or less Sriracha
- Use horseradish for an extra kick

1 glass

6 minutes

Chipotle Grapefruit Paloma

Ingredients:

- 2 oz tequila
- 1 oz fresh grapefruit juice
- 1/2 oz agave syrup
- Club soda
- Chipotle powder for rimming
- Grapefruit slice for garnish

Smoky Citrus: Chipotle Grapefruit Paloma
Experience the allure of smoky citrus with the Chipotle Grapefruit Paloma. Inspired by the vibrant streets of Mexico City, this cocktail marries the smokiness of chipotle with the tartness of grapefruit. It's a fiesta for your palate, a dance of flavors that lingers with every sip. Shake, pour, and let the smoky citrus celebration begin.

Directions

1. Rim the glass with chipotle powder.
2. In a shaker, combine tequila, grapefruit juice, and agave syrup.
3. Shake well with ice.
4. Strain into the glass over ice.
5. Top with club soda.
6. Garnish with a grapefruit slice.
7. Revel in the smoky citrus fiesta.

Substitutions

- Adjust sweetness with more or less agave syrup
- Use chili powder for a spicier rim

1 glass

10
minutes

Easy

Chili Mango Mojito

Ingredients:

2 oz white rum
1 oz fresh mango puree
3/4 oz simple syrup
1/2 oz fresh lime juice
6-8 fresh mint leaves
Chili slices for garnish

Origins & Popularity: The Chili Mango Mojito, a tropical escapade with a hint of spice, is inspired by the lively streets of Havana. Imagine the vibrant colors of vintage cars and the rhythm of salsa music as you sip this mojito. Crafted with the sweetness of mango and a kick of chili, this cocktail is a celebration of Cuban flavors. A dance of sensations awaits in every sip, a journey to the heart of Havana. Let the heat of the chili mingle with the coolness of mint for a thrilling experience.

Directions

1. In a shaker, muddle mint leaves with simple syrup.
2. Add rum, fresh mango puree, and fresh lime juice.
3. Shake well with ice.
4. Strain into a highball glass filled with ice.
5. Garnish with chili slices.
6. Picture yourself in the lively streets of Havana with each sip.
7. Feel the dance of sensations on your palate.
8. Cheers to the Chili Mango Mojito.
9. Enjoy the celebration of Cuban flavors.
10. Let the heat and sweetness create a thrilling experience.

Substitutions

-

1glass 8 minutes

Ginger Chili Whiskey Smash

Ingredients:

2 oz bourbon whiskey
3/4 oz ginger syrup
1/2 oz fresh lemon juice
1/4 oz chili-infused honey
Lemon wheel for garnish

Origins & Popularity: The Ginger Chili Whiskey Smash, a bold and spicy concoction, draws inspiration from the rugged charm of American whiskey bars. Picture a dimly lit speakeasy, the clink of ice in a glass, and the warmth of ginger and chili infusing the air. Crafted with the robust flavor of whiskey, this smash is a tribute to the rebellious spirit of the Prohibition era. With each sip, you'll feel transported to an era of secret indulgence and bold choices. A smash of flavors awaits.

Directions

1. In a shaker, combine bourbon whiskey, ginger syrup, fresh lemon juice, and chili-infused honey.
2. Shake well with ice.
3. Strain into a rocks glass filled with ice.
4. Garnish with a lemon wheel.
5. Picture yourself in a dimly lit whiskey bar with each sip.
6. Feel the bold and spicy infusion on your palate.
7. Cheers to the Ginger Chili Whiskey Smash.
8. Enjoy the rebellious spirit of the Prohibition era.
9. Let the robust flavors transport you to an era of secret indulgence.
10. Savor the smash of bold choices.

Substitutions

-

1glass

15 minutes

Spiced Cranberry Apple Cider

Ingredients:

2 oz spiced rum
3 oz apple cider
1 oz cranberry juice
1/2 oz cinnamon syrup
Apple slice and cinnamon stick for garnish

Origins & Popularity: The Spiced Cranberry Apple Cider, a comforting blend of autumnal flavors, is inspired by the crisp air and falling leaves of a New England harvest. Picture yourself by the fireside, wrapped in a cozy blanket, with a mug of this cider in hand. Crafted with the warmth of cinnamon and the tartness of cranberry, this drink is a celebration of the season. With each sip, you'll be transported to the heart of an autumn day, surrounded by the rich colors of nature. A comforting embrace awaits.

Directions

1. In a saucepan, heat apple cider, cranberry juice, and cinnamon syrup until warm.
2. In a mug, combine spiced rum with the warmed mixture.
3. Garnish with an apple slice and a cinnamon stick.
4. Picture yourself by the fireside with each sip.
5. Feel the comforting embrace of autumnal flavors.
6. Cheers to the Spiced Cranberry Apple Cider.
7. Enjoy the celebration of the season.
8. Let the warmth and tartness transport you to a New England harvest.
9. Savor the rich colors of nature in every sip.

Substitutions

-

1glass 12 minutes

Black Pepper Strawberry Collins

Ingredients:

2 oz gin
3/4 oz strawberry syrup
1/2 oz fresh lemon juice
1/4 oz black pepper tincture
Club soda, Strawberry slice for garnish

Origins & Popularity: The Black Pepper Strawberry Collins, a lively twist on a classic, is a nod to the bustling energy of a summer garden party. Picture the clinking of glasses, the laughter of friends, and the aroma of freshly picked strawberries in the air. Crafted with the sweetness of strawberries and the kick of black pepper, this Collins is a refreshing journey for the palate. With each sip, you'll feel the vibrancy of summer, a symphony of flavors that dance on your taste buds. A lively escape awaits.

Directions

1. In a shaker, combine gin, strawberry syrup, fresh lemon juice, and black pepper tincture.
2. Shake well with ice.
3. Strain into a highball glass filled with ice.
4. Top with club soda.
5. Stir gently.
6. Garnish with a strawberry slice.
7. Picture a summer garden party with each sip.
8. Feel the refreshing symphony of flavors.
9. Cheers to the Black Pepper Strawberry Collins.
10. Enjoy the lively twist on a classic.
11. Let the sweetness and kick create a vibrant escape.

Substitutions

-

1glass 5 minutes

Cinnamon Toasted Almond Cocktail

Origins & Popularity: The Cinnamon Toasted Almond Cocktail, a decadent treat with a hint of nostalgia, is inspired by the aroma of cinnamon toast in a cozy Bar. Picture a lazy Sunday morning, sunlight streaming through the window, and the comforting scent of cinnamon and almonds filling the air. Crafted with the richness of toasted almonds and the warmth of cinnamon, this cocktail is a sip of indulgence. With each sip, you'll be transported to a moment of sweet nostalgia, a toast to simplicity and decadence. An indulgent journey awaits.

Ingredients:

2 oz amaretto
1 oz cinnamon-infused simple syrup
1 oz heavy cream
Cinnamon stick for garnish

Directions

1. In a shaker, combine amaretto, cinnamon-infused simple syrup, and heavy cream.
2. Shake well with ice.
3. Strain into a rocks glass filled with ice.
4. Garnish with a cinnamon stick.
5. Picture a cozy Bar on a lazy Sunday morning with each sip.
6. Feel the decadent aroma of cinnamon and almonds.
7. Cheers to the Cinnamon Toasted Almond Cocktail.
8. Enjoy the sip of indulgence.
9. Let the richness and warmth transport you to a moment of sweet nostalgia.
10. Savor the toast to simplicity and decadence.

Substitutions

-

Chapter 7: Dessert Inspired

1 glass

5 minutes

Chocolate Martini

Ingredients:

- 2 oz vodka
- 1 oz chocolate liqueur
- 0.5 oz vanilla syrup
- 1 oz cream
- Chocolate shavings for garnish
- Ice

The Chocolate Martini, a sinfully indulgent creation, emerged from the glitz of the roaring '20s. A decadent blend of spirits and cocoa, it's an elegant homage to the timeless allure of chocolate.

Directions

1. In a shaker, combine vodka, chocolate liqueur, vanilla syrup, and cream.
2. Shake vigorously with ice.
3. Strain into a chilled martini glass.
4. Garnish with a sprinkle of chocolate shavings.

Substitutions

-

1 glass 8 minutes

Tiramisu Cocktail

Ingredients:

- 1.5 oz coffee liqueur
- 1 oz vanilla vodka
- 0.5 oz amaretto
- 1 oz mascarpone cheese
- 1 oz brewed espresso
- Ladyfinger crumbs for garnish
- Ice

The Tiramisu Cocktail, a spirited nod to the famed Italian dessert, captures the essence of coffee and mascarpone. A dessert in a glass, it elevates the art of mixology to the sublime.

Directions

1. In a shaker, combine coffee liqueur, vanilla vodka, amaretto, mascarpone cheese, and brewed espresso.
2. Shake well with ice.
3. Strain into a glass over ice.
4. Garnish with a sprinkle of ladyfinger crumbs.

Substitutions

-

1 glass

10
minutes

Key Lime Pie Daiquiri

Transport your taste buds to the Floridian coastline with the Key Lime Pie Daiquiri. A tropical twist on the classic, it marries the zing of key limes with the sweet melody of a dessert favorite.

Ingredients:

- 2 oz white rum
- 1 oz key lime juice
- 0.75 oz simple syrup
- Graham cracker rim
- Key lime wheel for garnish
- Ice

Directions

1. Rim the glass with graham cracker crumbs.
2. In a shaker, combine white rum, key lime juice, and simple syrup.
3. Shake well with ice.
4. Strain into the rimmed glass over fresh ice.
5. Garnish with a key lime wheel.

Substitutions

-

1 glass

7 minutes

Espresso Martini

The Espresso Martini, a caffeine-infused elixir born in the '80s London, brings together the worlds of coffee and cocktails. A bold and elegant libation that's a pick-me-up in more ways than one.

Ingredients:

- 2 oz vodka
- 1 oz coffee liqueur
- 1 oz freshly brewed espresso
- Coffee beans for garnish
- Ice

Directions

1. In a shaker, combine vodka, coffee liqueur, and freshly brewed espresso.
2. Shake well with ice.
3. Strain into a chilled martini glass.
4. Garnish with a few coffee beans for a touch of sophistication.

Substitutions

-

1 glass

5 minutes

Salted Caramel White Russian

Ingredients:

- 2 oz vodka
- 1 oz coffee liqueur
- 1 oz salted caramel syrup
- Cream
- Caramel drizzle for garnish
- Ice

The Salted Caramel White Russian, a modern twist on a classic, emerged from the creative depths of contemporary mixology. The marriage of velvety vodka and luscious caramel creates a decadent delight.

Directions

1. In a glass, combine vodka, coffee liqueur, and salted caramel syrup.
2. Add ice and top with cream.
3. Stir gently.
4. Drizzle caramel on top for an extra touch of sweetness.
5. Sip and savor the indulgence.

Substitutions

-

1 glass

8 minutes

Strawberry Shortcake Mimosa

Ingredients:

- 2 oz strawberry vodka
- 1 oz vanilla liqueur
- 3 oz chilled champagne
- Fresh strawberries for garnish
- Crushed shortbread cookies for rimming
- Ice cubes

Imagine the whimsy of a summer fair transformed into a cocktail—introducing the Strawberry Shortcake Mimosa. This effervescent delight, inspired by nostalgic fairs and sunny picnics, marries the sweetness of strawberries with the fizz of champagne. A sip of pure joy that's the perfect prelude to a delightful day.

Directions

1. Rim the glass with crushed shortbread cookies.
2. In a shaker, combine strawberry vodka and vanilla liqueur over ice.
3. Shake well and strain into the prepared glass.
4. Top with chilled champagne.
5. Garnish with fresh strawberries.
6. Sip, savor, and let the fairground magic unfold.

Substitutions

- Use plain vodka if strawberry vodka is unavailable.
- Experiment with different flavored liqueurs.
- Adjust sweetness with a touch of simple syrup if desired.

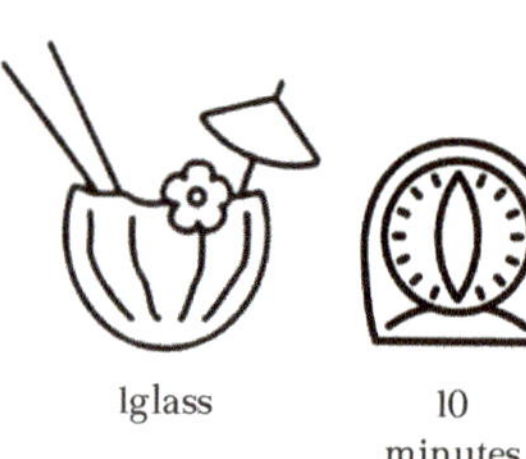

1glass

10 minutes

Banana Cream Pie Cocktail

The Banana Cream Pie Cocktail is a decadent ode to the classic dessert. Picture yourself in a vintage diner, the clink of forks against plates, and the aroma of freshly baked pie. This cocktail encapsulates those cherished moments, blending creamy banana goodness with a hint of nostalgia. It's dessert in a glass, a sip back in time.

Ingredients:

- 2 oz banana liqueur
- 1 oz vanilla vodka
- 1 oz coconut cream
- 1 oz half-and-half
- Graham cracker crumbs for rimming
- Banana slice for garnish
- Ice cubes

Directions

1. Rim the glass with graham cracker crumbs.
2. In a shaker, combine banana liqueur, vanilla vodka, coconut cream, and half-and-half over ice.
3. Shake well and strain into the prepared glass.
4. Top with ice cubes.
5. Garnish with a banana slice.
6. Sip slowly, indulging in the creamy nostalgia of banana cream pie.

Substitutions

- Substitute vanilla vodka with whipped cream vodka for extra richness.
- Use coconut milk as a dairy-free alternative.
- Adjust sweetness with a touch of simple syrup if desired.

1glass 12 minutes

Almond Joy Old Fashioned

Ingredients:

- 2 oz chocolate-infused bourbon
- 0.5 oz amaretto
- 1 sugar cube
- Angostura bitters
- Orange twist for garnish
- Almond shavings for garnish
- Ice cubes

The Almond Joy Old Fashioned is a sophisticated twist on the beloved candy bar. Born from the desire to elevate the classic cocktail, this creation combines the richness of chocolate, the nuttiness of almonds, and the warmth of bourbon. It's a sip-worthy symphony that pays homage to indulgence and tradition.

Directions

1. In a mixing glass, muddle the sugar cube with a few dashes of bitters.
2. Add chocolate-infused bourbon and amaretto.
3. Stir well to dissolve the sugar.
4. Strain into a glass with a large ice cube.
5. Express the oils from an orange twist over the drink.
6. Garnish with almond shavings.
7. Sip and savor the harmonious blend of chocolate, almonds, and bourbon.

Substitutions

- Infuse bourbon with chocolate by steeping cocoa nibs for a few days.
- Experiment with different flavored bitters.
- Adjust sweetness by adding more or less amaretto according to taste.

1glass

15 minutes

Raspberry Cheesecake Martini

Ingredients:

- 2 oz raspberry vodka
- 1 oz vanilla liqueur
- 1 oz heavy cream
- Fresh raspberries for garnish
- Crushed graham crackers for rimming
- Ice cubes

Indulge in the sheer decadence of the Raspberry Cheesecake Martini. Inspired by the elegance of a patisserie showcase, this cocktail combines the tartness of raspberries with the creamy allure of cheesecake. It's a sip that mirrors the sophistication of a dessert cart, promising a sublime experience for your taste buds.

Directions

1. Rim the glass with crushed graham crackers.
2. In a shaker, combine raspberry vodka, vanilla liqueur, and heavy cream over ice.
3. Shake vigorously.
4. Strain into the prepared glass.
5. Top with ice cubes.
6. Garnish with fresh raspberries.
7. Sip slowly, allowing the flavors to dance on your palate like a raspberry ballet.

Substitutions

- Experiment with raspberry-infused vodka for an extra burst of flavor.
- Substitute heavy cream with half-and-half for a lighter version.
- Adjust sweetness with a touch of simple syrup if desired.

1glass

10 minutes

Maple Pecan Bourbon Smash

The Maple Pecan Bourbon Smash is a celebration of autumnal flavors in a glass. Born from the crisp air of a fall day and the crunch of pecans underfoot, this cocktail weaves together the richness of bourbon, the warmth of maple, and the nutty delight of pecans. It's a toast to the season, inviting you to cozy up and savor the essence of fall.

Ingredients:

- 2 oz bourbon
- 1 oz pure maple syrup
- 0.5 oz pecan orgeat syrup
- 1 oz fresh lemon juice
- Pecan halves for garnish
- Rosemary sprig for garnish
- Ice cubes

Directions

1. In a shaker, combine bourbon, maple syrup, pecan orgeat syrup, and fresh lemon juice over ice.
2. Shake well.
3. Strain into a glass filled with ice.
4. Garnish with pecan halves and a rosemary sprig.
5. Sip slowly, embracing the autumnal symphony of maple and pecan.

Substitutions

- Make pecan orgeat syrup by combining pecans, sugar, and water in a blender.
- Experiment with different bourbons for diverse flavor profiles.
- Adjust sweetness by varying the amount of maple syrup according to taste.

Chapter 8: Garden Fresh

1 glass

5 minutes

Garden Gin and Tonic

Ingredients:

2 oz gin
4 oz tonic water
Fresh basil leaves
Cucumber slices
Ice cubes

Elevate your senses with the Garden Gin and Tonic, a botanical symphony of juniper and fresh herbs. Originating from Victorian gardens, this libation weaves tales of lush greenery and delicate flavors.

Directions

1. In a glass, muddle basil leaves and cucumber slices.
2. Fill the glass with ice cubes.
3. Pour in the gin.
4. Top with tonic water.
5. Gently stir to combine.
6. Garnish with a basil leaf. Sip and transport yourself to a Victorian garden party.

If you encounter a hiccup (perhaps an unexpected breeze), simply continue with step 6, gracefully stirring your way to botanical bliss.

Substitutions

-

1 glass

8 minutes

Basil Cucumber Cooler

The Basil Cucumber Cooler is a cooling elixir inspired by Mediterranean gardens. Refreshing cucumber dances with aromatic basil, creating a sip of sunshine.

Ingredients:

1 cucumber, peeled and sliced
8-10 fresh basil leaves
1 oz simple syrup
2 oz vodka
1 oz lime juice
Soda water
Ice cubes

Directions

1. In a shaker, muddle cucumber and basil with simple syrup.
2. Add vodka and lime juice. Shake well.
3. Strain into a glass with ice.
4. Top with soda water.
5. Stir gently.
6. Garnish with a basil leaf. Sip and be transported to a Mediterranean terrace.

If a citrusy breeze interrupts, calmly proceed with step 6, continuing your journey to refreshment.

Substitutions

-

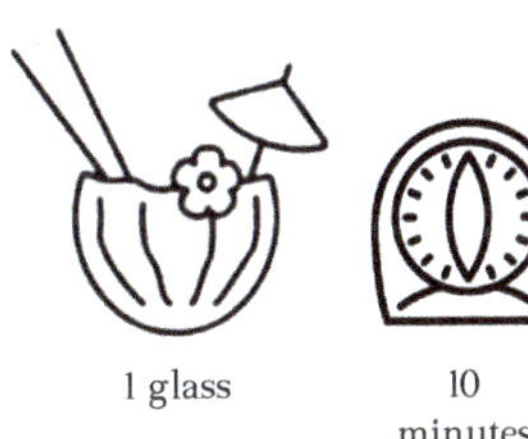

1 glass 10 minutes

Rose Petal Vodka Spritz

Indulge in the romance of the Rose Petal Vodka Spritz. With delicate petals and a hint of citrus, this concoction whispers tales of love and sophistication.

Ingredients:

2 oz vodka
1 oz rose syrup
1 oz elderflower liqueur
1 oz grapefruit juice
Sparkling water
Edible rose petals
Ice cubes

Directions

1. In a shaker, combine vodka, rose syrup, elderflower liqueur, and grapefruit juice. Shake well.
2. Strain into a glass with ice.
3. Top with sparkling water.
4. Garnish with edible rose petals. Sip and let the romance unfold.

Should a petal fall too soon, proceed with step 4, maintaining the enchantment.

Substitutions

Elderflower liqueur can be substituted.

1 glass

12 minutes

Beet Ginger Citrus Elixir

Embark on a vibrant journey with the Beet Ginger Citrus Elixir. Rooted in healthful beets and zesty citrus, this elixir rejuvenates both body and spirit.

Ingredients:

1 medium beet, peeled and diced
1-inch ginger, grated
1 orange, juiced
1 lemon, juiced
1 tbsp honey
Ice cubes

Directions

1. In a blender, combine beet, ginger, orange juice, lemon juice, and honey. Blend until smooth.
2. Strain into a glass with ice.
3. Stir gently.
4. Sip and feel the vibrant energy.

In case of a hiccup, calmly continue with step 4, savoring the healthful journey.

Substitutions

Honey can be substituted for agave syrup.

1 glass 7 minutes

Celery Thyme Collins

The Celery Thyme Collins is a crisp and herbal elixir inspired by garden simplicity. Fresh celery and thyme create a melody that's both invigorating and timeless.

Ingredients:

2 oz gin
1 oz celery juice
1 oz simple syrup
1 oz lemon juice
Fresh thyme sprigs
Soda water
Ice cubes

Directions

1. In a shaker, combine gin, celery juice, simple syrup, and lemon juice. Shake well.
2. Strain into a glass with ice.
3. Top with soda water.
4. Garnish with fresh thyme. Sip and embrace the garden in a glass.

Should a thyme leaf linger, proceed with step 4, maintaining the herbal harmony.

Substitutions

-

Tomato Basil Bloody Mary

Ingredients:

- 2 oz vodka
- 4 oz tomato juice
- 1/2 oz fresh lemon juice
- 1/4 oz simple syrup
- 1 dash hot sauce
- 1 pinch black pepper
- 2-3 fresh basil leaves
- Garnish: Celery stalk and cherry tomatoes

The Tomato Basil Bloody Mary, a brunch classic that traces its roots to the roaring 1920s. Picture this: the clinking of glasses and lively conversations. Legend has it that a savvy bartender in New York City elevated the humble tomato juice with basil, creating a symphony of flavors that became an instant sensation.
A nod to sophistication in every sip!

Directions

1. Muddle basil leaves gently in a shaker.
2. Add vodka, tomato juice, lemon juice, simple syrup, hot sauce, and black pepper.
3. Shake well and strain into an ice-filled glass.
4. Garnish with a celery stalk and cherry tomatoes. Revel in the timeless charm of this cocktail.

Substitutions

-

1glass

8 minutes

Arugula Pineapple Punch

Ingredients:

- 2 oz white rum
- 1/2 cup fresh pineapple chunks
- 1 handful arugula
- 1 oz simple syrup
- 1 oz lime juice
- Ice cubes
- Garnish: Arugula leaves and pineapple wedge

Allow me to introduce the Arugula Pineapple Punch, a libation inspired by lazy days on sandy shores. The peppery arugula meets the sweet caress of pineapple in a dance that will transport you straight to the beach. A sip, and you're seaside in your imagination!

Directions

1. Blend rum, pineapple chunks, arugula, simple syrup, and lime juice.
2. Strain into a glass filled with ice.
3. Garnish with arugula leaves and a pineapple wedge. Transport yourself to an island oasis with each delightful sip.

Substitutions

-

1glass

12 minutes

Carrot Orange Turmeric Twist

Enter the Carrot Orange Turmeric Twist, a vibrant concoction that celebrates health and flavor. Imagine a sunrise in a glass, with carrots and oranges leading the way. This drink, enriched with turmeric, is a testament to the joy of mindful sipping.
A burst of sunshine for your taste buds!

Ingredients:

- 1 cup carrot juice
- 1/2 cup fresh orange juice
- 1 oz ginger syrup
- 1/2 tsp ground turmeric
- Ice cubes
- Garnish: Orange slice and mint sprig

Directions

1. Shake carrot juice, orange juice, ginger syrup, and turmeric with ice.
2. Strain into an ice-filled glass.
3. Garnish with an orange slice and mint sprig.

Revel in the vibrant, invigorating embrace of this health-conscious elixir.

Substitutions

-

1glass 15 minutes

Bell Pepper Berry Breeze

Indulge in the vibrant symphony of the Bell Pepper Berry Breeze, where gin plays conductor to a medley of berries and the subtle heat of bell peppers. This concoction is a celebration of colors and flavors, a masterpiece in a glass.
A sensory journey for the adventurous palate!

Ingredients:

- 2 oz gin
- 1/2 cup mixed berries (strawberries, blueberries, raspberries)
- 1/4 cup diced red bell pepper
- 1 oz honey syrup
- 1 oz lime juice
- Ice cubes
- Garnish: Mixed berries and bell pepper slices

Directions

1. Blend gin, mixed berries, diced bell pepper, honey syrup, and lime juice until smooth.
2. Strain into a glass filled with ice.
3. Garnish with mixed berries and bell pepper slices.
Revel in the harmonious burst of flavors with each sip.

Substitutions

-

Super Hard

Zucchini Lemon Verbena Sling

Ingredients:

- 2 oz gin
- 1/2 cup sliced zucchini
- 1 oz lemon verbena syrup
- 1/2 oz elderflower liqueur
- 1 oz lemon juice
- Ice cubes
- Garnish: Zucchini ribbons and lemon verbena leaves

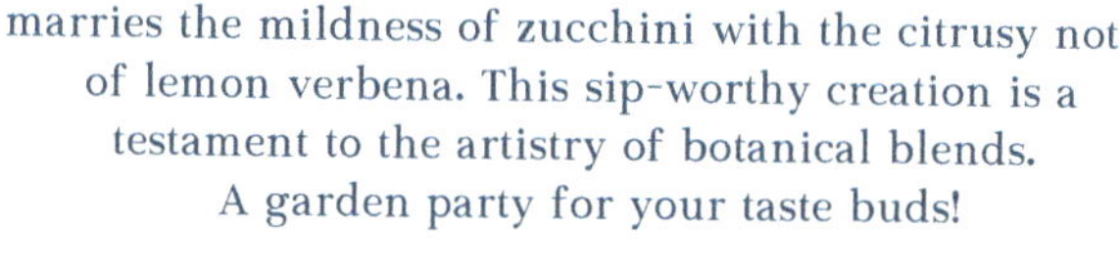

Elevate your cocktail experience with the Zucchini Lemon Verbena Sling, a garden-fresh marvel that marries the mildness of zucchini with the citrusy notes of lemon verbena. This sip-worthy creation is a testament to the artistry of botanical blends. A garden party for your taste buds!

Directions

1. Muddle sliced zucchini in a shaker.
2. Add gin, lemon verbena syrup, elderflower liqueur, and lemon juice.
3. Shake well and strain into a glass filled with ice.
4. Garnish with zucchini ribbons and lemon verbena leaves.

Immerse yourself in the intricate dance of botanicals with each sip.

Substitutions

-

Chapter 9: Sparkling Sips

1 glass

5 minutes

Easy

Classic Champagne Cocktail

Ingredients:

1 sugar cube
Angostura bitters
Chilled champagne
Lemon twist for garnish

Origins & Popularity: The Classic Champagne Cocktail, a timeless favorite, harkens back to the glamour of the early 20th century. Imagine the clinking of crystal glasses in a Gatsby-esque soirée, the bubbles of champagne mingling with a sugar cube. This cocktail is an ode to sophistication, a celebration in every effervescent sip. Crafted with the simplicity of champagne, sugar, and bitters, it's a journey to the elegance of a bygone era. Here's to the enduring allure of a classic.

Directions

1. Place a sugar cube in a champagne flute.
2. Dash the sugar cube with Angostura bitters.
3. Fill the flute with chilled champagne.
4. Garnish with a twist of lemon.
5. Picture a Gatsby-esque soirée with each sip.
6. Feel the bubbles mingle with the sophistication of a bygone era.
7. Cheers to the Classic Champagne Cocktail.
8. Enjoy the timeless allure of this effervescent classic.
9. Let each sip be a celebration of elegance.

Substitutions

-

1 glass

10 minutes

Elderflower Prosecco Punch

Ingredients:

3 oz prosecco
1 oz elderflower liqueur
1/2 oz fresh lemon juice
Club soda
Edible flowers for garnish

Origins & Popularity: The Elderflower Prosecco Punch, a delicate and floral concoction, draws inspiration from the meadows of Europe in spring. Picture a picnic under blooming elderflower trees, the air filled with their sweet fragrance. Crafted with the effervescence of prosecco and the subtle sweetness of elderflower liqueur, this punch is a toast to the beauty of nature. With each sip, you'll be transported to a sunlit garden, surrounded by the elegance of blossoms. A sip of spring awaits.

Directions

1. In a punch bowl, combine prosecco, elderflower liqueur, and fresh lemon juice.
2. Stir gently.
3. Top with club soda.
4. Pour into individual glasses filled with ice.
5. Garnish with edible flowers.
6. Picture a sunlit garden with each sip.
7. Feel the effervescence and sweetness of a blooming meadow.
8. Cheers to the Elderflower Prosecco Punch.
9. Enjoy the delicate and floral toast to nature.
10. Let each sip be a sip of spring.

Substitutions

-

1 glass

15 minutes

Sparkling Cranberry Apple Sangria

Ingredients:

3 oz sparkling white wine
2 oz cranberry juice
1 oz apple brandy
1/2 oz orange liqueur
Apple and cranberry slices for garnish

Origins & Popularity: The Sparkling Cranberry Apple Sangria, a festive and fruity blend, is inspired by the lively celebrations of autumn. Picture a harvest table adorned with the colors of cranberries and apples, laughter filling the air. Crafted with the vibrancy of sparkling wine and the tartness of cranberry, this sangria is a toast to abundance. With each sip, you'll be transported to a fall fiesta, surrounded by the warmth of friends and the richness of the season. A harvest celebration in every glass.

Directions

1. In a large wine glass, combine sparkling white wine, cranberry juice, apple brandy, and orange liqueur.
2. Stir gently.
3. Add ice to the glass.
4. Garnish with apple and cranberry slices.
5. Picture a harvest table with each sip.
6. Feel the vibrancy and tartness of cranberries and apples.
7. Cheers to the Sparkling Cranberry Apple Sangria.
8. Enjoy the festive blend of autumn.
9. Let each sip be a toast to abundance.

Substitutions

-

1 glass

8 minutes

Bellini Spritz

Ingredients:

2 oz peach puree
4 oz prosecco
Club soda
Peach slice for garnish

Origins & Popularity: The Bellini Spritz, a sparkling tribute to Italian elegance, is inspired by the sun-kissed orchards of peaches in Venice. Picture a waterfront café, the laughter of locals, and the aroma of ripe peaches. Crafted with the sweetness of peach puree and the effervescence of prosecco, this spritz is a sip of la dolce vita. With each sip, you'll be transported to the romantic charm of the Italian Riviera, a celebration of life. A sparkling journey awaits.

Directions

1. In a wine glass, add peach puree.
2. Top with prosecco.
3. Add ice to the glass.
4. Top with club soda.
5. Stir gently.
6. Garnish with a peach slice.
7. Picture a waterfront café in Venice with each sip.
8. Feel the sweetness and effervescence of peaches.
9. Cheers to the Bellini Spritz.
10. Enjoy the sparkling tribute to la dolce vita.
11. Let each sip be a celebration of the Italian Riviera.

Substitutions

-

1 glass

12 minutes

Sparkling Watermelon Mint Agua Fresca

Origins & Popularity: The Sparkling Watermelon Mint Agua Fresca, a refreshing and hydrating delight, is a tribute to summer's bounty. Picture a sun-soaked picnic, the sound of children's laughter, and the juiciness of ripe watermelon. Crafted with the crispness of sparkling water and the invigorating freshness of mint, this agua fresca is a sip of summer. With each sip, you'll be transported to a carefree afternoon, surrounded by the simplicity and joy of the season. A sip of sunshine awaits.

Ingredients:

2 cups watermelon cubes
6-8 fresh mint leaves
1 oz simple syrup
4 oz sparkling water
Ice cubes
Mint spring for garnish

Directions

1. In a blender, combine watermelon cubes, fresh mint leaves, and simple syrup.
2. Blend until smooth.
3. Strain the mixture into a glass filled with ice.
4. Top with sparkling water.
5. Stir gently.
6. Garnish with a mint sprig.
7. Picture a sun-soaked picnic with each sip.
8. Feel the juiciness and freshness of ripe watermelon and mint.
9. Cheers to the Sparkling Watermelon Mint Agua Fresca.
10. Enjoy the refreshing delight of summer.
11. Let each sip be a sip of sunshine.

Substitutions

-

1 glass 5 minutes

Champagne Pomegranate Fizz

The Champagne Pomegranate Fizz, a effervescent symphony that marries the sophistication of champagne with the ruby allure of pomegranate.

Ingredients:

- 4 oz champagne
- 1 oz pomegranate juice
- 0.5 oz simple syrup
- Pomegranate seeds for garnish
- Ice

Directions

1. In a flute, pour champagne.
2. Add pomegranate juice and simple syrup.
3. Stir gently.
4. Add ice.
5. Garnish with pomegranate seeds.
6. Sip and savor the bubbly dance of flavors.

Substitutions

-

1glass

7 minutes

Limoncello Sparkler

The Limoncello Sparkler, a radiant burst of Italian sunshine in a glass, blending the zesty charm of limoncello with the effervescence of soda.

Ingredients:

- 2 oz limoncello
- 4 oz club soda
- 0.5 oz simple syrup
- Lemon twist for garnish
- Ice

Directions

1. In a highball glass, combine limoncello, club soda, and simple syrup.
2. Add ice.
3. Stir gently.
4. Garnish with a twist of lemon.
5. Enjoy the refreshing embrace of this citrus-infused libation.

Substitutions

-

1glass

8 minutes

Sparkling Pear Rosemary Refresher

The Sparkling Pear Rosemary Refresher, a fragrant ode to the seasons, intertwining the sweetness of pear with the aromatic whisper of rosemary.

Ingredients:

- 2 oz pear nectar
- 4 oz sparkling water
- 0.75 oz rosemary simple syrup
- Pear slices for garnish
- Ice

Directions

1. In a glass, combine pear nectar, sparkling water, and rosemary simple syrup.
2. Add ice.
3. Stir gently.
4. Garnish with pear slices.
5. Revel in the harmonious blend of fruit and herb.

Substitutions

-

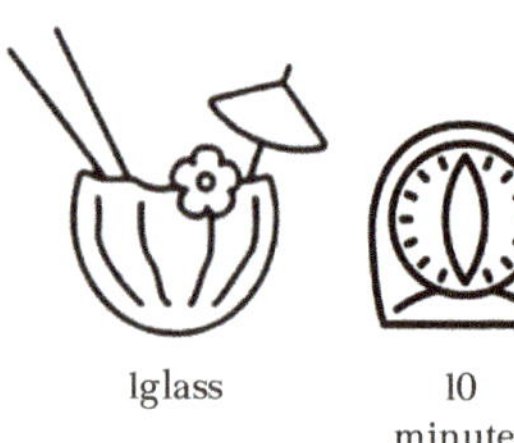

1glass

10 minutes

Ginger Beer Hibiscus Sparkle

The Ginger Beer Hibiscus Sparkle, a lively concoction marrying the spiciness of ginger beer with the floral elegance of hibiscus.

Ingredients:

- 2 oz hibiscus tea, cooled
- 4 oz ginger beer
- 0.5 oz honey
- Lemon wheel for garnish
- Ice

Directions

1. In a glass, combine hibiscus tea, ginger beer, and honey.
2. Add ice.
3. Stir gently.
4. Garnish with a lemon wheel.
5. Experience the invigorating fusion of flavors in every effervescent sip.

Substitutions

-

1glass 15 minutes

Cranberry Orange Champagne Float

The Cranberry Orange Champagne Float, a festive cascade of flavors, merging the tang of cranberry with the citrusy embrace of orange and the elegance of champagne.

Ingredients:

- 2 oz cranberry juice
- 1 oz orange liqueur
- 4 oz champagne
- Orange zest for garnish
- Vanilla ice cream
- Ice

Directions

1. In a glass, combine cranberry juice, orange liqueur, and champagne.
2. Add ice.
3. Top with a scoop of vanilla ice cream.
4. Garnish with orange zest.
5. Delight in the effervescent celebration of flavors.

Substitutions

-

Chapter 10: Whimsical Creations

1 glass

10 minutes

Easy

Blue Lagoon

Dive into the azure allure of the Blue Lagoon, a cocktail born from the coastal charm of the Caribbean. This enchanting libation, featuring a harmonious blend of blue curaçao, vodka, and lemonade, captures the essence of a tropical oasis. Close your eyes, take a sip, and let the waves of flavor transport you to sun-kissed shores.

Ingredients:

- 2 oz vodka
- 1 oz blue curaçao
- 3 oz lemonade
- Lemon wheel for garnish
- Ice cubes

Directions

1. Fill a shaker with ice.
2. Add vodka and blue curaçao.
3. Shake well to chill.
4. Strain into a glass filled with ice.
5. Top with lemonade.
6. Garnish with a lemon wheel.
7. Sip, savor, and imagine the gentle lull of the Caribbean sea.

Substitutions

- Experiment with flavored vodkas for a unique twist.
- Adjust sweetness by varying the amount of blue curaçao.

1 glass

15 minutes

Easy

Unicorn Punch

Ingredients:

- 4 oz sparkling wine
- 2 oz mixed fruit juices (pineapple, orange, and cranberry)
- 1 oz elderflower liqueur
- Edible glitter for garnish
- Ice cubes

Step into the realm of whimsy with the Unicorn Punch, a magical concoction inspired by the fairy tales of childhood. This kaleidoscope of flavors, featuring sparkling wine, fruit juices, and a hint of mystery, promises a sip that sparkles and dances on your palate. Pour yourself a glass, and let the enchantment begin.

Directions

1. In a glass, combine sparkling wine, mixed fruit juices, and elderflower liqueur over ice.
2. Stir gently to mix.
3. Garnish with edible glitter for a touch of magic.
4. Sip slowly and let the enchanting flavors unfold.

Substitutions

- Use any combination of your favorite fruit juices.
- Substitute elderflower liqueur with peach schnapps for a different twist.

1 glass

12 minutes

Easy

Fairy Tale Fizz

Ingredients:

- 2 oz gin
- 1 oz lavender syrup
- 1 oz fresh lemon juice
- Sparkling water
- Lavender sprig for garnish
- Ice cubes

Embark on a journey through flavors with the Fairy Tale Fizz, a cocktail inspired by the pages of storybooks. This effervescent delight, featuring gin, lavender syrup, and sparkling water, is a sip of pure fantasy. Close your eyes, take a sip, and let the floral notes and bubbles transport you to a land where tales come to life.

Directions

1. In a shaker, combine gin, lavender syrup, and fresh lemon juice over ice.
2. Shake well to chill.
3. Strain into a glass filled with ice.
4. Top with sparkling water.
5. Garnish with a lavender sprig.
6. Sip and let the floral fizz weave its magic on your senses.

Substitutions

- Make a non-alcoholic version by omitting the gin.
- Experiment with different herb-infused syrups.
- Adjust sweetness with a touch of simple syrup if desired.

1 glass

8 minutes

Galaxy Martini

Journey into the cosmos with the Galaxy Martini, a celestial creation that marries the rich hues of the universe with the elegance of a classic martini. Vodka, blackberry liqueur, and a touch of magic combine to create a sip-worthy galaxy in your glass. Take a sip, and let the stars dance on your palate.

Ingredients:

- 2 oz vodka
- 1 oz blackberry liqueur
- 0.5 oz simple syrup
- Edible glitter for rimming
- Lemon twist for garnish
- Ice cubes

Directions

1. Rim the glass with edible glitter for a cosmic touch.
2. In a shaker, combine vodka, blackberry liqueur, and simple syrup over ice.
3. Shake well to chill.
4. Strain into the prepared glass.
5. Garnish with a lemon twist.
6. Sip slowly, gazing at the celestial wonders in your glass.

Substitutions

- Experiment with different flavored vodkas for a cosmic twist.
- Substitute blackberry liqueur with crème de cassis for a different berry note.

1 glass

10 minutes

Enchanted Forest Elixir

Immerse yourself in the mystical allure of the Enchanted Forest Elixir, a potion that draws inspiration from the secrets hidden within ancient woods. With gin, green chartreuse, and a touch of woodland magic, this cocktail is a sip of fantasy. Take a journey through the enchanted woods with every flavorful drop.

Ingredients:

- 2 oz gin
- 0.75 oz green chartreuse
- 0.5 oz fresh lime juice
- 0.5 oz simple syrup
- Fresh mint leaves for garnish
- Ice cubes

Directions

1. In a shaker, combine gin, green chartreuse, fresh lime juice, and simple syrup over ice.
2. Shake well to chill.
3. Strain into a glass filled with ice.
4. Garnish with fresh mint leaves.
5. Sip and let the enchanting flavors transport you to a magical woodland realm.

Substitutions

- Experiment with different herbal liqueurs for a diverse forest flavor.
- Adjust sweetness with a touch of honey syrup if desired.

1 glass 7 minutes

Easy

Magical Mule

Ingredients:

2 oz vodka
4 oz ginger beer
1 oz lime juice
1 tsp simple syrup
Mint leaves
Ice cubes

The Magical Mule is a potion born from the whimsy of mystical lands. With ginger's warm embrace and the sparkle of citrus, it enchants the senses.

Directions

1. In a copper mug, combine vodka, lime juice, and simple syrup.
2. Fill the mug with ice cubes.
3. Top with ginger beer.
4. Stir gently.
5. Garnish with mint leaves. Sip and let the magic unfold.

Should a magical creature interrupt, simply continue with step 5, stirring your way to enchantment.

Substitutions

-

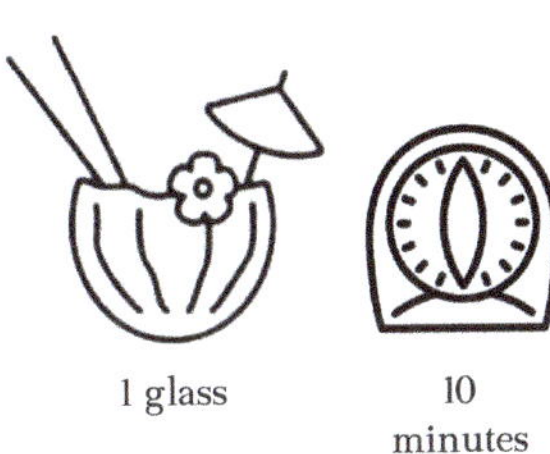

1 glass

10 minutes

Wonderland Whirl

The Wonderland Whirl, a fantastical elixir inspired by Lewis Carroll's tales. Raspberry sweetness twirls with the zing of citrus, creating a journey down the rabbit hole.

Ingredients:

2 oz gin
1 oz raspberry syrup
1 oz lemon juice
1 egg white
Fresh raspberries
Ice cubes

Directions

1. In a shaker, combine gin, raspberry syrup, lemon juice, and egg white. Shake vigorously.
2. Strain into a glass with ice.
3. Garnish with fresh raspberries. Sip and fall into the wonderland of flavors.

If a Cheshire Cat distracts, continue with step 3, savoring the whimsy.

Substitutions

Raspberry syrup can be substituted.

1 glass 8 minutes

Mystical Margarita

Ingredients:

2 oz tequila
1 oz triple sec
1 oz agave syrup
1 oz lime juice
Orange twist
Salt (for rimming)
Ice cubes

The Mystical Margarita, a tequila symphony that dances between sweet and tangy. Born on the shores of mystery, it captures the essence of a sun-kissed siesta.

Directions

1. Rim a glass with salt.
2. In a shaker, combine tequila, triple sec, agave syrup, and lime juice. Shake well.
3. Strain into the prepared glass with ice.
4. Garnish with an orange twist. Sip and let the mystery unfold.

In case of a sunbeam distraction, calmly continue with step 4, embracing the siesta vibes.

Substitutions

Agave syrup can be substituted.

1 glass

12 minutes

Cosmic Cooler

Ingredients:

1 oz blue curaçao
1 oz coconut rum
1 oz pineapple juice
1 oz orange juice
Pineapple wedge
Maraschino cherry
Ice cubes

The Cosmic Cooler, a celestial concoction inspired by the vastness of the universe. Blue curaçao orbits with tropical fruits, creating a sip of intergalactic bliss.

Directions

1. In a shaker, combine blue curaçao, coconut rum, pineapple juice, and orange juice. Shake well.
2. Strain into a glass with ice.
3. Garnish with a pineapple wedge and a maraschino cherry. Sip and soar into the cosmic abyss.

If a shooting star interrupts, continue with step 3, riding the cosmic wave.

Substitutions

-

1 glass

15 minutes

Normal

Starlight Sangria

The Starlight Sangria, a constellation of flavors that illuminates any gathering. Red wine embraces a medley of fruits, creating a cosmic celebration in every sip.

Ingredients:

4 oz red wine
1 oz brandy
1 oz orange liqueur
1 oz orange juice
Mixed berries (blueberries, raspberries, strawberries)
Orange slices
Sparkling water
Ice cubes

Directions

1. In a pitcher, combine red wine, brandy, orange liqueur, and orange juice.
2. Add mixed berries and orange slices. Refrigerate for at least 2 hours.
3. Before serving, top with sparkling water and ice cubes.
4. Pour into glasses and marvel at the starlit infusion.

In case of a meteor shower, continue with step 4, toasting to cosmic wonders.

Substitutions

Brandy can be substituted for rum.

Chapter 11: Mocktail Marvels

1 glass 8 minutes

Virgin Mojito

Ingredients:

- 8 fresh mint leaves
- 1 oz simple syrup
- 1 oz lime juice
- 1/2 cup club soda
- Ice cubes
- Garnish: Mint sprig and lime wedge

The Virgin Mojito, a mocktail that traces its roots to the vibrant streets of Havana, Cuba. In the 16th century, local indigenous ingredients blended with Spanish flair, giving birth to this refreshing concoction. Now, it graces glasses worldwide, a testament to its timeless appeal. A sip of history in every glass!

Directions

1. In a glass, muddle mint leaves with simple syrup and lime juice.
2. Fill the glass with ice cubes.
3. Top with club soda and gently stir.
4. Garnish with a mint sprig and a lime wedge.

Savor the refreshing zest of this timeless classic.

Substitutions

-

1 glass

10 minutes

Berry Basil Lemonade

Ingredients:

- 1/2 cup mixed berries (strawberries, blueberries, raspberries)
- 1 oz fresh basil leaves
- 1 oz simple syrup
- 2 oz lemon juice
- 1 cup cold water
- Ice cubes
- Garnish: Mixed berries and basil leaves

The Berry Basil Lemonade, a harmonious blend born in the sun-kissed orchards of the Mediterranean. Imagine a citrus symphony with a berrylicious twist and the herbal grace of basil. This mocktail, a toast to leisurely afternoons, has found its way to hearts worldwide. A melody of flavors for your taste buds!

Directions

1. In a blender, combine mixed berries, basil leaves, simple syrup, and lemon juice.
2. Blend until smooth.
3. Strain into a glass filled with ice.
4. Top with cold water and stir.

Garnish with mixed berries and basil leaves.
Revel in the symphony of refreshing flavors.

Substitutions

-

1 glass

5 minutes

Cucumber Mint Cooler (Non-Alcoholic)

Ingredients:

- 1/2 cucumber, sliced
- 5-6 fresh mint leaves
- 1 oz simple syrup
- 1 oz lime juice
- 1 cup sparkling water
- Ice cubes
- Garnish: Cucumber slice and mint sprig

Introducing the Cucumber Mint Cooler, a mocktail that redefines cool sipping. Originating from the spa culture of ancient Rome, where health and refreshment intertwined, this concoction carries the crispness of cucumber and the invigorating punch of mint. A spa day for your taste buds!

Directions

1. In a glass, muddle cucumber slices and mint leaves with simple syrup and lime juice.
2. Fill the glass with ice cubes.
3. Top with sparkling water and stir gently.
4. Garnish with a cucumber slice and mint sprig.

Enjoy the revitalizing embrace of this spa-inspired creation.

Substitutions

-

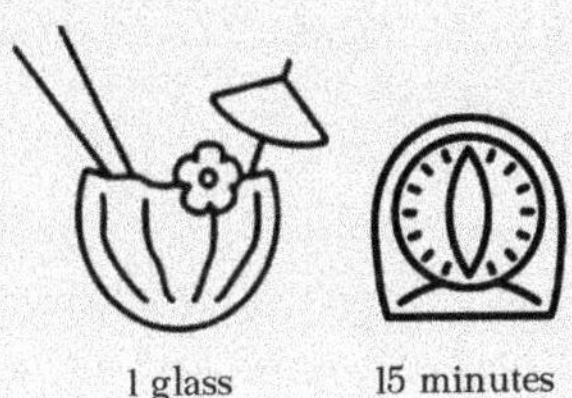

1 glass 15 minutes

Tropical Virgin Punch

Ingredients:

- 1/2 cup pineapple juice
- 1/2 cup mango juice
- 1 oz orange juice
- 1 oz grenadine
- 1 cup coconut water
- Ice cubes
- Garnish: Pineapple wedge and mint sprig

The Tropical Virgin Punch, a non-alcoholic symphony inspired by the lush landscapes of the tropics. Picture yourself on a beach, the sun setting, and this vibrant concoction in hand. Pineapple, mango, and citrus dance together in this mocktail masterpiece.
A tropical escape in every sip!

Directions

1. In a shaker, combine pineapple juice, mango juice, orange juice, and grenadine.
2. Shake well and strain into a glass filled with ice.
3. Top with coconut water and stir gently.
4. Garnish with a pineapple wedge and mint sprig.

Transport yourself to a tropical paradise with every sip.

Substitutions

-

1 glass 12 minutes

Virgin Watermelon Margarita

Ingredients:

- 1 cup fresh watermelon cubes
- 1 oz lime juice
- 1 oz simple syrup
- 1/2 oz orange juice
- Salt for rimming
- Ice cubes
- Garnish: Watermelon wedge and lime wheel

The Virgin Watermelon Margarita, a tequila-free fiesta that echoes the spirit of lively Mexican celebrations. Crafted with the sweetness of watermelon and the zing of citrus, it's a toast to joyous moments. ¡Salud to a mocktail fiesta!

Directions

1. In a blender, combine watermelon cubes, lime juice, simple syrup, and orange juice.
2. Blend until smooth.
3. Rim a glass with salt.
4. Fill the glass with ice and pour the blended mix.
5. Garnish with a watermelon wedge and lime wheel.

¡Enjoy the fiesta of flavors!

Substitutions

-

1 glass

10
minutes

Sparkling Pineapple Mint Mocktail

Origins & Popularity: The Sparkling Pineapple Mint Mocktail, a tropical sensation, transports you to the sun-drenched beaches of the Caribbean. Picture swaying palm trees, the gentle lapping of waves, and the refreshing aroma of pineapple. Crafted with the sweetness of pineapple juice and the invigorating freshness of mint, this mocktail is a sip of paradise. With each sip, you'll be transported to an island getaway, surrounded by the simplicity and joy of the tropics. A mocktail vacation awaits.

Ingredients:

2 oz pineapple juice
4 oz sparkling water
Fresh mint leaves
Pineapple wedge for garnish

Directions

1. In a glass, combine pineapple juice and sparkling water.
2. Add fresh mint leaves.
3. Stir gently.
4. Fill the glass with ice.
5. Garnish with a pineapple wedge.
6. Picture sun-drenched beaches with each sip.
7. Feel the sweetness and freshness of pineapple and mint.
8. Cheers to the Sparkling Pineapple Mint Mocktail.
9. Enjoy the tropical sensation.
10. Let each sip be a sip of paradise.

Substitutions

-

Virgin Strawberry Bellini

Ingredients:

2 oz strawberry puree
4 oz sparkling water
Fresh strawberries for garnish

Origins & Popularity: The Virgin Strawberry Bellini, a delightful berry twist, is inspired by the lush strawberry fields of summer. Picture a sunlit orchard, the fragrance of ripe strawberries, and the laughter of friends. Crafted with the lusciousness of strawberry puree and the effervescence of sparkling water, this mocktail is a celebration of berries. With each sip, you'll be transported to a berry-filled fiesta, surrounded by the sweetness and joy of the season. A berry celebration in every glass.

Directions

1. In a champagne flute, add strawberry puree.
2. Top with sparkling water.
3. Stir gently.
4. Garnish with fresh strawberries.
5. Picture a sunlit orchard with each sip.
6. Feel the lusciousness and effervescence of strawberries.
7. Cheers to the Virgin Strawberry Bellini.
8. Enjoy the delightful berry twist.
9. Let each sip be a berry-filled fiesta.

Substitutions

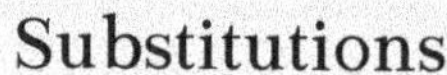

-

1glass 12 minutes

Blueberry Lavender Lemonade (Non-Alcoholic)

Ingredients:

2 oz blueberry syrup
4 oz lemonade
1/2 oz lavender syrup
Fresh blueberries and lavender sprigs for garnish

Substitutions

-

Origins & Popularity: The Blueberry Lavender Lemonade, a floral and fruity melody, is inspired by the enchanting fields of blueberries and lavender. Picture a serene garden, the aroma of lavender in the air, and the burst of blueberries. Crafted with the tanginess of lemonade, the sweetness of blueberries, and the floral notes of lavender, this mocktail is a sip of tranquility. With each sip, you'll be transported to a peaceful garden, surrounded by the calming essence of lavender and the vibrancy of blueberries. A sip of serenity awaits.

Directions

1. In a glass, combine blueberry syrup, lemonade, and lavender syrup.
2. Stir gently.
3. Fill the glass with ice.
4. Garnish with fresh blueberries and lavender sprigs.
5. Picture a serene garden with each sip.
6. Feel the tanginess and sweetness of blueberries and the calming essence of lavender.
7. Cheers to the Blueberry Lavender Lemonade.
8. Enjoy the floral and fruity melody.
9. Let each sip be a sip of tranquility.

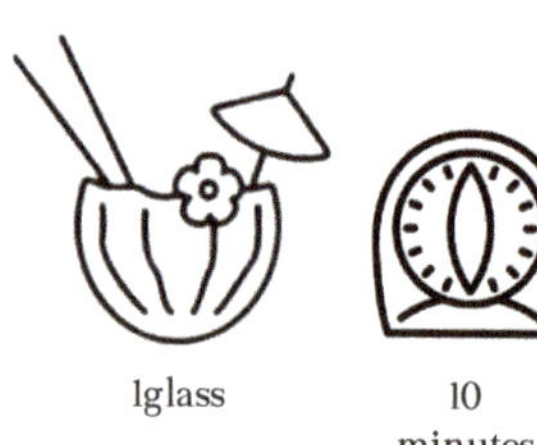

1glass

10 minutes

Citrus Mint Sparkler (Non-Alcoholic)

Origins & Popularity: The Citrus Mint Sparkler, a zesty and refreshing creation, is inspired by the sun-kissed citrus groves of Mediterranean summers. Picture a vibrant orchard, the citrusy aroma filling the air, and the coolness of mint. Crafted with a medley of citrus juices and the invigorating freshness of mint, this mocktail is a burst of sunshine. With each sip, you'll be transported to a citrus-filled paradise, surrounded by the zing of citrus and the coolness of mint. A sip of Mediterranean bliss awaits.

Ingredients:

2 oz orange juice
1 oz grapefruit juice
1 oz lemon juice
4 oz sparkling water
Fresh mint leaves for garnish

Directions

1. In a glass, combine orange juice, grapefruit juice, and lemon juice.
2. Stir gently.
3. Fill the glass with ice.
4. Top with sparkling water.
5. Stir gently.
6. Garnish with fresh mint leaves.
7. Picture a vibrant citrus grove with each sip.
8. Feel the zing and freshness of citrus.
9. Cheers to the Citrus Mint Sparkler.
10. Enjoy the zesty and refreshing creation.
11. Let each sip be a burst of sunshine.

Substitutions

-

1glass 8 minutes

Virgin Raspberry Mint Julep

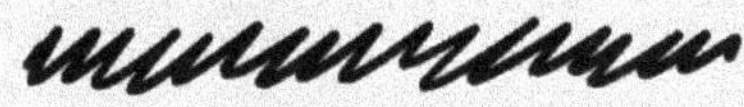

Origins & Popularity: The Virgin Raspberry Mint Julep, a berry-infused delight, pays homage to the classic Southern cocktail. Picture a charming porch, the gentle rustle of leaves, and the sweetness of raspberries. Crafted with the vibrancy of raspberry puree and the invigorating coolness of mint, this mocktail is a sip of Southern charm. With each sip, you'll be transported to a breezy porch, surrounded by the sweetness and hospitality of the South. A berry-infused sip awaits.

Ingredients:

2 oz raspberry puree
4 oz crushed ice
Fresh mint leaves for muddling and garnish

Directions

1. In a glass, muddle fresh mint leaves.
2. Add raspberry puree.
3. Fill the glass with crushed ice.
4. Stir gently.
5. Garnish with fresh mint leaves.
6. Picture a charming porch with each sip.
7. Feel the sweetness and hospitality of the South.
8. Cheers to the Virgin Raspberry Mint Julep.
9. Enjoy the berry-infused delight.
10. Let each sip be a sip of Southern charm.

Substitutions

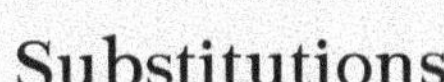

-

We have a small favor to ask

In the spirited symphony of shakers, muddlers, and the tantalizing dance of spirits, youve embarked on a libation adventure with Quick & Easy Mixology. From classic concoctions to inventive elixirs, weve stirred and shaken our way to crafting the perfect cocktails, all captured in this liquid journey.

As the last drop settles in your glass, Im not here to bid adieu but to extend an invitation. In the realm of small publishers, reviews are the hidden gems that glitter in the dimly lit corners of the literary landscape.

So, my fellow mixologist, if the essence of our cocktail craft has stirred something in your soul, let your voice be the garnish on this literary libation. Navigate back to the digital watering hole where you quenched your thirst for mixological wisdom. Seek out that oft-overlooked review button - a humble vessel awaiting your impressions.

A rating, a sentence, a fleeting moment of your time - its the zest that elevates our concoction from mere liquid to an experience shared. For small publishers like us, your review is the ripple that turns into a tidal wave of recognition, a toast to the passionate pursuit of mixological perfection.

In the hallowed halls of our creative endeavor, each review is a cherished sip of appreciation. We read them with the same meticulous attention we give to balancing flavors in a cocktail. Your thoughts, whether a harmonious symphony or a note of critique, resonate deeply with us.

And, my friend, if you chance upon a small hiccup, a misplaced ingredient in our literary cocktail, know that weve juggled the bottles with care, striving for excellence. Mistakes, like spilled drops, can occur, but we hope your palate is forgiving.

Your review isnt just a parting gesture; its an enduring legacy in the narrative of our mixological escapade. So, as you set down the glass and close the chapter, consider this not just a request but an expression of gratitude for being part of our spirited journey.

In conclusion, my fellow cocktail enthusiast, cheers to the shared love of mixology and the moments weve stirred together. Your review is the final garnish, the twist of citrus that brightens our creative concoction. May your drinks be well-mixed, your spirits high, and your reviews as memorable as the perfect cocktail.

www.ingramcontent.com/pod-product-compliance
Ingram Content Group UK Ltd.
Pitfield, Milton Keynes, MK11 3LW, UK
UKHW062004290726
14090UKWH00022B/1373

9 798869 328113